MEMORY LANE

BY

Henry M. Parnes

MEMORY LANE
HENRY M. PARNES

Copyright 2021

Book typography and production by Dave Bricker

ISBN: 978-0-578-85339-0

for my wife and life-partner Sonia.
She claims not to be my muse,
but there's no doubt she is.
She urges me on,
inspires me with her own prose,
and is there for me
as a sounding board
and wise counsel
in so many more ways
than mere words can tell.

Table of Contents

1

Preface

We are always drawn to Memory Lane
From wherever future trails take us;
For Memory is what transports us back
To the firm, familiar glimpses of Yesteryear.

This, my personal anthology, entitled *Memory Lane*, is a collection of short stories which were written at various times,
mostly in response to monthly themes defined by the South
Florida Writers' Association.

This august body of writers, of which I am a proud member,
made it possible for me to distill and direct my writing talents to
the required topic. You, my esteemed reader, will be the judge as
to whether I was worthy of the many prize-winning accolades
bestowed upon me.

A good half of my stories are very personal; I write about events and situations I encountered at various stages during my long life. I encourage you to pay particular attention to them, so that you can better get the measure of the intimate and varied experiences which shaped me.

The other stories I also hope you will find enlightening. I've done my best to entertain myself in writing them. By doing so, I fervently hope that you will enjoy reading them.

Sincerely,

Henry M. Parnes
Hialeah, Florida
January 2021

1

The Six-Day War Remembered
(June 5–10, 1967)

I t's been more than fifty years since the violent, cataclysmic, armored confrontation called the Six-Day War, but the memories of it will be seared and embedded in my deepest recollections for as long as I live.

I was there. I played a vital role in a small nation's desperate battle for its continued existence, against overwhelming odds.

We were outnumbered in every way. The Egyptian military had a standing army much larger than ours, and had almost twice as many first-line battle tanks. They had far more artillery pieces, far more planes — fighter jets, fighter-bombers, and helicopters — than we. And once you include the Jordanian forces, the Syrian military, and elements of Iraqi, Saudi and Lebanese combatants, you realize the impossibility of Israel's task. They were all lined up against us, to slaughter us or drive us into the Mediterranean Sea.

Any serious, professional military strategist would conclude that we didn't stand a chance against the combined Arab might arrayed against us. But one vital ingredient was in our favor: Our troops were tough, well-trained, and self-reliant. We were brave, with a cussed determination to overcome all odds, even though we were fighting with our backs against the wall — or maybe because of it.

The conflict began when Egyptian strongman Nasser moved two armored divisions into the relatively quiet Sinai Peninsula; the Sinai acted as a buffer between Israel and her most intractable enemy, Egypt. Nasser wanted to unite the Arab nations under his leadership. This show of force was his way of demonstrating that he meant business against the hated "Zionist entity," Israel.

In response, Israel called up a couple of reserve force divisions, mostly armored. My tank brigade was among the first to be removed from civilian life and sent out to the Egyptian border.

The average Israeli citizen lives like a volunteer fireman. When there's a perceived threat to the country, they drop everything in civilian life and rush to their army base. For front-line tank commanders like me, this meant being transported to one of Israel's several red-hot borders to meet the threat head-on.

This call-up was my third of that year, 1967. The previous two had involved missions of short duration. The first was at the Jordanian border where our tanks and infantry went in to clear out some Fedayeen who were using a Jordanian border village to launch raids into Israel, threatening farming communities.

I was back home in three days. The second involved an intensive four-day training session in the Negev Desert, where we honed our skills as tankers.

But Nasser's illegal incursion was different. By entering the Sinai, the deployed Egyptian armored divisions cut Israel's only commercial maritime connection to Africa, Australia, and the Far East. The other sea route through the Suez Canal had been blocked to Israeli shipping for many years.

The Egyptians were intent on closing the noose by isolating and suffocating Israel.

It was mid-May; Israel had just celebrated her Independence Day with a military parade, which we had attended. A day or so later, well after midnight, I was pulled out of bed by a hard rapping on our front door. My infant daughter was asleep in the adjacent room.

The terse instructions handed to me by a reserve soldier were for me to report to my armored brigade's home base, somewhere south of Tel Aviv. My wife promised to call my employer and inform them of my call-up. Within half-an-hour, I was on the road, buoyed by goodbye kisses, a chicken sandwich, and a bottle of water.

Upon arrival at my base, I met with old friends and made new ones. Every year, soldiers completed their military service. They returned to civilian life, but during national emergencies many were called back to the bases where they had served their regular army service. We knew our tanks inside out because every year after discharge we had been called back to sharpen our skills on reserve duty.

I knew the procedure. Over at the requisitions warehouse, we changed into army fatigues and stowed our civilian clothing. The reality started sinking in. As a tank commander, I was presented with a list of things to check, and supplies to requisition. It didn't take long for us to get our supplies and equipment together.

We tank commanders and our crews walked over to our assigned tanks, which were housed in large corrugated metal sheds. Our tank would be our home-away-from-home for the duration of this latest challenge to our national existence.

We understood that we had been called up as a precaution, until things returned to normal in the Sinai Peninsula. The Israeli High Command expected the United Nations to tell Nasser to pull back his armored divisions. This never happened.

Our commanding officer was a "take-charge" military leader who knew how to get what he wanted.

"This looks serious," he said. "There haven't been any tanks in the Sinai since the Suez War of '56. The U.N. has imposed a ban on armor and howitzers since then, so we believe that Nasser is spoiling for a war."

We surmised that this confrontation would involve a lengthy wait at the border until the U.N. got the Egyptians to back off. The insertion of Egypt's armed forces directly threatened another member nation—Israel—and that was in violation of the United Nations charter.

Our tanks were transported on flatbeds most of the way to the Egyptian border. We were bused there. At a staging area, we took possession of our tanks and the remainder of our equipment. Under cover of darkness, we drove to our forward positions a short distance from the Egyptian border.

For the next two weeks we settled into our desert home.

With tensions rising, we kept busy. Our tanks were camouflaged under finely woven netting. From a few yards away, our tanks looked like undulating sand mounds in the desert. Underneath the netting, as the insufferable heat and the ubiquitous flies permitted, we went over battle readiness maneuvers.

Even though this was the era of transistor radios, we learned little about what was going on with the concentration of forces. We learned that Israel's Foreign Minister was doing the rounds among sympathetic Western democracies, but this resulted in platitudes and little else. There was some talk of organizing an international flotilla to break the impasse, but nothing came of it.

A continuous stream of military and civilian vehicles flowed around our emplacements. (In a national emergency, civilian trucks and buses are requisitioned along with their drivers.) Reinforcements arrived constantly. Civilian life in Israel ground to a halt.

In the cities and towns, the elderly were inducted into a Home Guard. The young, primarily high-schoolers, were assigned to fill sandbags and dig trenches in Israel's populated areas. In the cities, windows were boarded up. Women assumed duties as diverse as milking cows, delivering mail, and driving city buses.

We learned that the Egyptian armored divisions had "parked" themselves just across the border from us, together with supporting infantry divisions and artillery.

We maintained strict radio silence apart from coded inter-division messages. From the other side we heard a constant stream of Arabic voices over the airwaves, and those of the Russian officers were there in numbers to assist the Egyptians.

A short distance away, mere minutes on a fast-moving tank, lay the Egyptian border. We joked that some of our designated "shit-holes" were probably close enough to the Egyptians for them to smell our waste if the wind was blowing in their direction.

"Well, if that's the situation," I joked, "we're going to win the smell war. Our shit must smell a lot worse than theirs. Compare what we're being fed to the special, deluxe, Russian meals which are flown in for their side."

During daylight hours, our outside activities were restricted. We made an effort to keep our forward positions hidden from the prying border overflights conducted by Russian and Egyptian pilots.

An exception was made when portable shower stalls were brought in periodically. In the desert, showers were something special that we all looked forward to.

As a prelude to the war, a couple of aerial dogfights took place in the skies above us, which we followed with considerable interest. The Israel Air Force came through unscathed, while four Russian—made MiG 21s crashed into the ground. One fighter jet, streaming black smoke, spiraled down and spectacularly exploded just a few kilometers from our forward positions. Some of our officers sped off in a command car to examine the wreckage, and confirm that it was a Russian MiG.

Suddenly, unbelievably, we received news that we were going home to our loved ones! The Israeli High Command had decided that our brigade, as a bonus for being called up to be among the very first forces, would receive an "After Duty" leave of approximately eighteen hours—a brief trip home after almost three weeks at the border. The world press showed pictures of Israeli soldiers on leave enjoying themselves on the beach, though this may also have had a deceptive, relaxing effect on Cairo, Damascus, and Amman.

At home, I found myself in a dream. Coming up my street and climbing the familiar steps to my apartment; my eyes caressed every remembered scene. My wife threw herself at me in delight, commenting on how dusty I appeared, and how I had lost weight.

I cooed over my sleeping seven-month-old daughter, and wondered whether I would ever see her grow up.

What a luxury to sleep in a soft bed in close contact with a loved one! We went over to my mother-in-law's for a meal. The family was pretty depleted because almost every one of my wife's brothers had been called up for reserve army duty. The only one still home was Phillip, my wife's younger brother. He had a gimpy leg caused by childhood polio, but even he was out digging trenches.

The time came too quickly for me to return to the front. As I gathered my beret, my jacket, and my Uzi sub-machine gun, I faced my wife and little girl, and put up a brave front, reassuring my wife that all would be well. I'm not sure she believed me.

I knew there was only one solution to the threat of being choked by Egypt's dictator, and that was to defeat his forces in battle. This wasn't going to be easy; Syria and Jordan had entered into a military alliance with Egypt. The task facing us was formidable.

June 4th: few people envisioned what was about to happen.

The sun was setting as our trucks filled with returning tank crewmen arrived at our hidden forward positions. The Egyptian and Russian spy planes probably saw many tank tracks on their reconnaissance missions, but we made it difficult for them to identify exactly what their pictures revealed.

Certainly, they saw a lot of military vehicles scattered around the terrain, but where was Israel's strike force?

After dark we were visited by our division's commanding officer, General Arik Sharon. Portly with a mop of devil-may-care tousled hair, he wore baggy pants and was widely respected as a great military strategist.

There must have been almost a thousand of us gathered to hear him speak. He scrambled onto the hood of his jeep and told us that the war was about to begin, and that our battle plan was to fight deep inside Egyptian territory.

"We're going to shock them. They are going to be confused and panic-stricken." The general put his hand down into his pants. "They think we're gonna come in like this…" he jerked his extended hand forward— "but we're gonna hit 'em from *here* 'n' *here* 'n' *here*." He yanked his arm and hand forward in his pants to emphasize the movements of attack. We cheered wildly.

Sharon continued, hoarse from previous speeches. "Our Air Force will clear the way for you as you move forward. Our paratroopers will take care of a lot of the enemy's resistance before you reach their embedded defensive positions. The Germans called this 'Blitzkrieg.' We'll strike like lightning. They won't stand a chance."

General Sharon's positive assessment of the military situation left us enthusiastic about the outcome. His entourage moved him on to his next audience, which had gathered to hear him speak a few kilometers away in the blanketing darkness opposite the enemy.

Back in our tanks, the activity and preparation became intense. I checked every aspect of my tank's battle readiness, going over every check-list item with my crew.

An officer appeared out of the darkness and called me aside to tell me the latest news.

"Instruct your crew to be ready for action at the crack of dawn. Finish your preparations and get your crew to sleep—fully clothed, boots on…. A runner will wake you at oh-three-hundred. Then report to the command center immediately for the latest instructions."

He disappeared into the enveloping gloom, going from tank to tank with his news.

❧

I was awakened by a nameless guard. None of us had slept well that night, but I was dozing when the guard shook my boot and told me to report to the command center.

I wriggled out of my tight sleeping bag. Shivering in the early-morning breeze, I pulled on a sweater. Shouldering my sub-machine gun, I stepped over the deep tank-track ruts that criss-crossed the wild terrain and headed over to the deeply entrenched half-track which was the communications headquarters of the brigade.

The moon had already set behind the low desert hills in front of our positions. As I stumbled forward, a flashing light blinked momentarily a little to my right.

I jogged toward it, stumbling as I ran, and reached the covered entrance of the half-track. Other figures, unidentifiable in the dark, joined me. Throwing the flap open, we descended into the decline leading to the underground vehicle. The pit was large. Soldiers were everywhere.

A powerful light was beamed from above, and a forest of ever-changing silhouettes danced in a discordant ferment. Though everyone tried to speak quietly, it was loud inside. Squinting, I greeted several of my fellow commanders, among them Ben-Attia and Ilan Shapiro, who had been in NCO school with me during my regular army stint years before.

Ben-Attia slapped my back, smiling. "Congratulate me; I'm a father to a brand-new baby boy, Jonathan."

I gave him a hug. His eyes sparkled. "The announcement just came over brigade communications. I guess in the excitement of seeing me leave for the front, my Shoshana's water broke and my mother rushed her to the hospital."

Ilan Shapiro raised his voice above the cacophony. "We'll get together after all this craziness is over, to celebrate."

The three of us nodded in agreement.

A powerful spotlight came on, illuminating a large map against the packed-sand wall. Our brigade commander stepped onto an ammunition box in front of the map and raised his hands to ask for silence. He was a vigorous, unquenchable man with black hair just turning grey around the temples; he held the rank of colonel at the tender age—for colonels—of forty-one. We admired and respected him.

"*Chev'reh*, guys, Our time has come—our time to strike out for freedom from oppression. We've dragged you away from your jobs, your careers. This is serious business.

"In a very short time, we will be at war. Half an hour ago, the Egyptians opened fire on several of our border kibbutzim near the Gaza Strip. Their targets were civilians—innocent men, women, and children."

He looked around, searching for our eyes. "A generation ago, in Nazi Europe, our people were helpless, at the mercy of those butchers, with no place to go, no place to find protection. Now we have a nation, our own country. We must do everything in our power to provide this protection…."

"We are going to war because the Egyptians are trying to choke us. *We will not be choked!* We'll be fighting for our lives, and the lives of our wives and sweethearts, for our children and our parents, for our friends, for one another, for our nation, for our freedom. We must overcome, because we cannot afford to lose."

He looked around, his tongue grazing his lips. "We are a small nation, few in number, but we have a dynamic, swift army. Our battle plan is simple: We will thrust deep into enemy territory to carry the fight into the heart of the Sinai, and beyond if need be.

"Unlike them, we don't intend to murder civilians, or rape women, or burn and plunder. We'll break through their armored fortifications, cut their lines of supply and communications, and drive all the way to the Suez to destroy their reserve forces."

We broke into applause, but he raised his hands—his face deadly serious—to cut us off.

"Our supply lines will be stretched. What does a tanker do when he runs out of shells? *He does what is necessary to get re-supplied…!*" He looked around him, nodding slowly. "If you encounter mechanical problems, sit tight until help arrives.

"You tank commanders are our elite—our strike force. We're counting on you. Stay out of trouble. Keep in touch with one another to minimize casualties. But this is war. Soldiers die during wars. So fight like there's no tomorrow, so we'll all have a lot of tomorrows."

Ben-Attia and I exchanged quick, meaningful glances. The cold, ugly, metallic scowl of Death had entered our midst, had become part of our struggle for survival.

The colonel sensed Death's incursion and tried to quash it. "I know this isn't easy for you. Most of you guys are Reserve Non-Commissioned Officers. You're getting on with your lives. Many of you are married. Some of you have children. Ben-Attia, where are you?"

Ben-Attia raised his hand high, pumping his fist. The colonel shielded his eyes against the glare and pointed at him. "Ben-Attia over there is a brand-new father, as of this morning. He and his wife have their first baby, a boy."

The assembly erupted in a resounding *"mazel tov."*

The colonel continued. "After all this is over, and we return to base, we'll celebrate his baby's arrival…. As I was saying, we all have someone special to go home to. This … this interruption in our lives has to be dealt with. And then we can return to living our lives, hopefully in peace, for a long time to come."

The colonel shuffled, changed his footing on the ammunition box. He began to speak, wordlessly mouthing something, stopped, then began again. "I'd like to personally wish every one of you Godspeed and the very best of luck. I'll be in touch with you over our radio network once we move forward. Are there any questions?"

No one spoke; even the jokers among us remained silent.

"*Beseder*—are all tanks and their crews battle-ready? If not, report to the sergeant-major at the exit, before you leave…. One last important thing: When you see my half-track above ground, I'll be waving a large red flag. That's your signal to lift up your tails and go!

"Dismissed."

We filed out of the huge hole underneath the camouflaged tent and climbed up to see the wonder of dawn gradually breaking over the bleak, undulating landscape. A brisk breeze blew east-to-west, toward the Egyptian border. The sun lifted its life-giving, fiery glow above the horizon, inspecting and illuminating the earth below. A few fast-moving birds flitted by, their wings beating and trilling in unison. The ubiquitous pesky flies were back, seeking moisture where they could find it.

On my way back to my tank, I thought about what the colonel had said. We were fighting for the survival of our nation. Our country was counting on us, willing us to victory. I thought of my wife, baby daughter and my mother-in-law; it wasn't easy for them either. I wondered what it was like for them, worrying about me, a long way from the front lines.

At least here we knew that we'd be battling the enemy in a short while. "Fight like hell, and don't get into trouble." That's what the colonel had said.

My crew was waiting for me, wide-awake, nervous, and anxious for news. We had expected the assault to begin at dawn. I explained everything I knew about the situation, and got them to continue their preparations.

Things were coming to a head.

"When does a war start?" I asked them rhetorically.

"It starts when the generals decide it'll start, and not before."

I went over what awaited us to keep their minds occupied.

With our driver, I rechecked the fuel gauge.

With our gunner, I checked the shells and examined the stored belts of bullets for our machine gun.

I asked every member of the crew to check their Uzis and their cartridges.

We practiced retrieving, loading, aiming, and firing shells. We prided ourselves at our heightened rate of firing.

I checked on reserves of water and rations.

I checked the first-aid kit.

I examined the interior of the tank, ensuring that everything was in place and operational.

We were a well-oiled machine, ready for the impending conflict.

Our enthusiasm peaked and ran headlong into our lack of sleep.

The heat added to our discomfort.

The crew settled into the shady side of our tank's netting.

At seven–forty, a runner came by, instructing us to raise the netting onto the tank, "rev" up the engine, and take up battle-stations.

This was it.

The time had arrived.

The heat was oppressive; the sun was now high in the sky.

I opened the hatches to invite a little breeze inside. I sat in my commander's hatch looking back toward the command center. Nothing yet.

My driver looked over to me with that question in his eyes.

I shouted, above the booming rumble of our tank. "Remember what I told you, Natan: A war doesn't begin until the generals decide."

His dark eyes stared back at me. "This is a hell of a time to start a war, in the middle of the day!"

(Only after the war was over would we discover the real reason why the war started when it did.)

I shrugged.

The minutes ticked by slowly.

We were nervous and jumpy: sweat poured down my forehead onto my goggles and headset.

At precisely eight o'clock, my crew turned on a transistor radio and listened to the newscast of the Voice of Israel. It was difficult to hear over the loud thrum of our tank engines. The female newscaster was her usual cool self as she read the news of the day. Her disembodied voice was a tiny oasis of calm in a madly boiling world.

She offered no word of anything unusual, just ordinary, humdrum happenings in a world too preoccupied with itself to sense the growing storm.

At five after eight, a high-pitched roar approached from behind my right shoulder. The noise actually drowned out our tank's thrum.

I looked back, and observed an amazing sight: Silver aluminum Israeli birds of prey— fighter jets and fighter-bombers—flew in from the north-east, glistening in the morning sunshine.

Flying low—probably between fifty to seventy-five feet above ground—they incredibly dipped their wings in salute and sped on, rumbling, hungry for their targets. The roaring thunderclap of their finely-tuned engines was overwhelming.

I concentrated on one plane in particular, furiously waving my arm and looking at the pilot. He saw me and raised his palm. As he thundered out of view, I caught a glimpse of his "thumbs up" signal.

We felt an intense pride in those brave pilots. Tears welled in our eyes. Those sleek birds of war were our avenging angels.

"*Give 'em hell!*" we shouted above the exploding ru
engines. The ground shuddered and vibrated wit
pearing shock wave.

A relative quiet followed. Only our growling engi
silence.

By now they must be well into enemy territory.

Long seconds passed. Then, from beyond the horizon, came
the cacophonous *Whump! Whump! Whump! Whump!* of muffled
explosions.

I looked back.

The colonel's half-track had plowed to the top of the hole. His
red flag waved briskly.

"*Go!*" I yelled, turning on my radio and adjusting my headset.

In bustling New York, it was a few minutes after 1:00 a.m.

In swinging London and illuminated Paris, dawn was just
breaking....

Our tanks drove fast over unfamiliar terrain, moving toward
the enemy, churning up clouds of dust.

We were at war for the third time in twenty years. We were at
war to undo the strangling noose around our necks; we were a
small nation, but we needed room to breathe, to survive, to pros-
per, just as other nations can.

❧

The war was over. There were still a number of mopping-up operations in progress, but the back of Egypt's fighting force had been broken, its vaunted legions and weaponry smashed by Israel's furious, unrelenting *blitzkrieg*.

The Israeli Air Force's brilliantly-executed, coordinated bombing of at least *eighteen* military air bases had destroyed most of Egypt's attack aircraft on their runways. This was done in the first hours of the war; our planes first bombed the runways with special concrete-penetrating bombs, and then systematically mangled the planes themselves.

The Israeli Army's strategic planners discovered a 'chink' in Egypt's armor—their Achilles Heal - which largely decided the war. They found out that patrolling warplanes' pilots changed their on-duty shifts at between eight to eight-thirty every morning. That was the time, the Israeli Air Force concluded, when the great majority of Egypt's warplanes were grounded—the perfect time to strike. *And strike they did*; eighteen different Egyptian airfields all over Egypt and the Sinai were struck at precisely the same time, eliminating all but a few of their front-line planes.

❧

My tank was only bothered twice by air attacks during the entire campaign; on both occasions, the MiG 21s—among the very few which were able to take off and attack Israeli forces—strafed us, but their pilots had so many targets to choose from, it reminded me of a single mosquito among a crowd of plump nudists: *where does he go from here?*

My tank was involved in so much that in the years since the Six-Day War I have etched each and every encounter with the enemy to memory; *where* and *when* we fired shells, and against *which* tanks or emplacements, and where we were geographically.

I remember that during the first night, in the middle of a Russian-designed 'killing field,' my tank and others from our brigade ran out of shells. Predicting this, I had radioed ahead, asking for re-supply. A truck loaded with shells arrived, but couldn't get close enough to us because of the terrain and the enemy firestorm.

I noticed that the Egyptian shelling was rotational; the bombardment had swung away from us to another area in the enclosed valley.

"*Quick!*" I yelled at my crew. "*Follow me!*" We scrambled out of our tank, and I started a hand-to-hand chain from the truck to our tank illuminated by bursts of shelling, ours and theirs.

On the last scramble with the shells, we were caught between the supply truck and our tank as the enemy bombardment swung back to our area.

I yelled at my crew. *"Down! Drop the shells! Dig for dirt!"*

I desperately dug with my fingernails, trying to create a little shallow trench for my body. I heard shells exploding close by, and shrapnel whizzing past my ears. I remember promising God (and believe me, I'm not religious!) as my life hung in the balance, exposed and vulnerable, that I would go to temple and give thanks for coming through unscathed. (Upon my fortuitous arrival home, I fulfilled this.)

Eventually, we were successful in continuing to fire until their canons were silenced.

The following morning, an amazing event occurred, something that our people had been praying for, for the past two thousand years. As I was instructing my crew to grab their 'mess-tins' and go to an arriving mobile field kitchen for breakfast, someone from a nearby communications truck blurted out, *"the Western Wall is Ours! We've retaken the Old City!"*

As I wrote, I'm not religious: never have been. Proud to be Jewish, proud of our contributions to the Arts, to Culture, to Science, to Medicine, to life itself. But King Solomon's Western Wall, once again in our hands, that's *really something*, well beyond mere religion.

A day later, after breaking the back of the Egyptians' defensive positions—designed by the Russians—our tank brigade was involved in a wild headlong race in the dark to reach the Mitla and Gidi Passes through the Sinai Mountains. The passes were the Egyptian military's only escape route to get to the Suez Canal and across the bridges to safety in Egypt.

Our tank was in the middle of a mass of other tanks, both Egyptian and Israeli, galloping across the desert side-by-side, plowing up clouds of dust in pitch blackness. We didn't know whether the tanks on either side of ours were Israeli or Egyptian. There was a humorous episode during that long night. The Egyptian tankers were constantly chatting with one another. I guess they were encouraging one other after being bludgeoned by our blitzkrieg: they were fleeing for their lives. One of my crew was from Egypt: he spoke Arabic with the distinctive Egyptian dialect. I gave him my headphones, and he translated what they were saying. I asked him to participate in their conversation.

He told them that the hated Israelis had special deadly weaponry in their tanks and planes, and that there was no way to avoid their shells and rockets but to welcome Death. It was psychological warfare of the first magnitude.

After a half an hour of banter, he launched into a spate of the spiciest of Arabic swear words: there was a silence of a few seconds before the individual Egyptian tankers realized that they had been duped by an Arab-speaking Israeli, and they responded in kind. The airwaves must have positively sizzled!

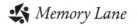

In the very first light of dawn, while everything outside of our tanks was still a murky haze, we received curt instructions to wheel around and commence firing on any vehicle that was identifiably Egyptian. We chose a slight incline to the side of the Mitla pass. Many Israeli tanks made for that location, which offered a superb view of all traffic headed for the pass.

One after another, sometimes in exploding volleys, Egyptian tanks were hit and caught fire. We had a side-on view of vehicles desperate to get to Mitla. It was like shooting fish in a barrel.

Much later we took stock. The colonel was dead: a shell had ripped through his half-track during a successful confrontation with superior enemy forces.

Ben-Attia of the quiet smile and happy-go-lucky attitude was dead too: an Egyptian shell had smashed into his tank turret. He never saw his newborn baby boy. His Shoshana became a widow in an agonizing instant.

❧

The day was beautiful: pleasantly hot, just a few clouds in the sky. On the scorched earth, the view was not a pretty one. Blackened, burned-out hulks were everywhere. Tired, unshaven and haggard, with not more than a precious few hours' sleep in the previous four days, we had reached an asphalted road — *what luxury*! I told my driver to stop beside two blackened Russian-built hulks. The tarmac around them was still liquid from the intense heat.

More to relieve myself than anything else, I jumped from my tank and walked around the nearer smoldering wreck; I stumbled upon the corpse of a man, lying on his back. Every part of him had been burned, first by being in the tank when it received a direct hit, and finally, after dying, he had been burned and puffed by the harsh desert sun.

His hands were extended, his fingers bent in as if trying to grasp something. His eyes, glazed and deathlike, were open. On the second finger of his left hand I could see a partially melted wedding band.

I looked at him, and something in me snapped. I felt an intense feeling of compassion for the man. He had been married. Probably somewhere in an Egyptian city his wife waited anxiously for his return. He continued to stare up at the sky, looking out at all creation with his unseeing eyes, asking unanswerable questions.

Why, oh why, I asked myself, do we have to fight wars? Can't we resolve territorial disputes by negotiation? Wouldn't it be far better to live in peace with one another, to build, to create?

That burned corpse could have been any one of us. It could, but for a far kinder fate, have been me.

Extreme sleeplessness, futility and an overwhelming sadness overcame me. I looked at the dead Egyptian, and I wept for all the colonels and the Ben-Attias—all the good men who were no more.

2

Almost Stranded in a Foreign Land

*T*he day had begun pretty much like any other. I had slept
soundly, even though in the dark recesses of my mind I
knew that day was Travel Day; those days for me were usually
burdensome and filled with stress and urgency. All about making
sure that I had packed everything, that I had remembered my
travel documents, that I had the necessary financial and insurance brochures and application forms I would need.

I would be flying to Curacao, in the Netherland Antilles, off the
coast of Venezuela, where by good fortune I had many faithful
clients. My securities and insurance practice had expanded out
of my office in Miami, and now included many clients in diverse
communities all through the Americas and the Caribbean basin.

I owed my expansion into these locales to a friendship with a
rabbi who had been referred to me by a chance encounter several
years earlier.

Like many of the well-to-do and cautiously wary upper classes in Latin America, the rabbi had a *pied-a-terre* in Miami. Through him I was introduced to many people from 'down south' who were in need of financial assistance. When these people came to Miami, many of them were invited to my home and my office. My client-base was now quite diverse, spread into many countries.

In order to cater to these remote clients, I found it both necessary and very lucrative to travel for one week every month, to Mexico, or to various Central and South American countries as well as to the Caribbean Basin. I planned the trips so that I came home generally on Thursdays or Fridays with new applications and clients' funds intended for securities, investments and insurance.

On this particular occasion, I was scheduled to spend four days in Willemstad, the biggest town on Curacao and the then-capital of the Netherlands Antilles.

The time to leave for the airport came, with all of the incumbent stresses and inconveniences. I bade goodbye to my then-wife and two daughters, telling them that I would be home on the following Friday, latest.

By the time I got on the plane, I was frazzled. Checking in, passport, ticket. Watching my suitcase disappear on a conveyorbelt. Baggage inspection; travel document examination; duty-free items purchased for key clients. Arriving at the gate. Nonchalantly finding a seat, with my roll-on's handle extended in front of me. Waiting tentatively for the plane's arrival. Deplaning passengers. Boarding announcements. The inevitable shuffle. Going down the boarding ramp, my roll-on, my constant companion, rolling along with me. Being welcomed by the long-suffering, smile-at-all-costs airline stewardesses. Finding my seat, my roll-on faithfully squeezing down the aisle behind me. Waiting for other passengers to pass by. Finally, grunting, lifting my roll-on into the stowage bin above my head.

Middle seats were thankfully empty; like many other travelers, I don't appreciate being squeezed or packed too tightly. I struck up a conversation with an older, balding man in the window seat. *He seems pleasant enough;* I found out that he was the regional manager for a large international hotel chain. I told him that I was staying at his company's hotel while in Curacao. We shook hands; he introduced himself as Leon Bookman.

Our friendly chatter encouraged a younger man wearing glasses, serious demeanor, sitting across the aisle from me to join in. He told the two of us that he was the Caribbean sales manager for a refrigeration company. Introduced himself as Mitchell Blomberg. We shook hands.

By the time we were served drinks, the three of us had become fast friends. On my trips, I'd found that normally closed-mouth individuals became downright loose-lipped. With a cocktail or two, or something harder (not for me, for them; I normally settle for some white wine), we were talking about our wives and our children. Found out that Leon was a grandfather, divorced, divorced again and presently with his third wife. Reasonably happy with his lot.

Mitchell (he refused to be called 'Mitch': said that it cheapened his name) was on his way to Curacao to supervise the installation of new air conditioners for the government buildings in Willemstad.

Chatting happily with my two new-found friends, the flight seemed a short one. Before we realized it, the pilot was announcing our approach to Willemstad Airport. I found out that we were all scheduled to leave three days hence, on the same Miami-bound flight: a happy coincidence.

Leon was staying at the same hotel I was: Mitchell had reservations for a tony Bed-and-Breakfast close to the Parliament Buildings. Before we parted outside of the airport terminal, we agreed to meet for a drink at a well-known coffee shop and bar after work; Leon proposed the venue.

Leon and I caught a cab and checked in to the hotel. He used his influence to upgrade me to a junior suite, in spite of my protestations. He said that he had influence, and why not take advantage of it?

I made four or five phone calls. The first was to inform my then-wife that I had arrived safely.

She mentioned that a tropical storm had developed in the eastern Caribbean, and told me to be aware of it. The other calls were to clients, setting up appointments at the hotel for the following day.

That evening, when the three of us met in the fashionable and exotic downtown Punda area, not far from the Government Buildings, the topic of the storm came up. Leon opined that even if it developed into a hurricane, it would probably keep well to the north of Curacao, in 'Hurricane Alley,' and that hurricanes very rarely veered so far south as to threaten the island. "I wouldn't worry about it," he said confidently.

"Still, we should be aware that it's in the general area," uttered Mitchell, taking a sip of his coffee. "All of the AC units are sitting in their boxes outside the Parliament, waiting for our crews to haul them inside. Be a real balls-up if bad weather hits them."

"Could you cover them with a tarp, to protect them?" I suggested helpfully.

"*Many* tarps," said Mitchell. They're in a secure fenced-in outdoor location, but we'd need many more tarps than we have."

Leon chipped in. "Just to be on the safe side, I'd suggest that you cover them securely."

"That's exactly it. How do you lash them down if a 'cane comes through here…. It's something that I never considered."

"They say that hurricanes are pretty rare this far south."

"But they *do* happen, and this one may be the one which bucks the trend."

Leon disappeared into the bowels of the café, and came back a few minutes later. He looked worried. "Just checked with a friend of mine. Works in the meteorological department here in Curacao. He told me that this tropical storm is now close to being a Cat One hurricane, and it's continuing along on its unusual southward path. Advised me to err on the side of caution and see whether we could get out of here earlier than Friday."

Mitchell knit his brow. "I can't leave until those AC units are installed."

"What's more important to you—the lives of your installers and *your* life, or some friggin' air conditioners?"

"I'll make a call to the airline," I suggested.

I came back a few minutes later with the negative reply written all over my face. "They told me that they were fully booked, and the other two carriers don't have seats either."

Leon shrugged. "Well, let's look on the bright side. It's probably going to veer again and scoot north across to the 'Hurricane

Alley' and miss us entirely. Then all we have to worry about is that the pilot avoids it on the way home."

Between us, we decided to go for dinner at a fish-and-local-specialties restaurant which Leon had recommended, in a former plantation house on the other side of Willemstad. The meal was sumptuous. I enjoyed the unusual ambiance of the weathered old building on a cliff overlooking the ocean and the banter with my two new friends, but it left me wondering whether we were doing the right thing by staying on the island.

"What about flying *south* — to Caracas, for instance?" I posited. "That way at least we'd be safely out of the storm's path."

"Uh-uh," Leon clucked. "Even further away from home? That wouldn't be a good idea."

"Just thinking of all the potential escape routes," I countered.

By the following morning, the newly-created Category One hurricane was on everyone's lips. The storm now had a name: Hurricane Joan. And it was continuing on its southern path, coming directly toward Curacao, hugging the northern coast of South America.

I was in the hotel dining room waiting for Leon to join me. A couple of American tourists, an elderly intrepid pair, were talking loudly about what they should do about the impending arrival of the storm. "I would suggest that we just stay where we are," the man said. "This building is probably as safe a place as any on the island."

"If you say so," the woman added. "I just get nervous when I hear that a hurricane is coming."

Leon slid into his chair opposite mine. "'mornin,'" he grunted. "We're gonna get *hit*, that's fairly certain. It *could* veer slightly to the north, but even then, we'd still be in its sphere of influence. My meteorologist friend just confirmed it. It's all a case of how close it comes to the island. The good news is that it's *dawdling*: he says that we could start feeling the effects probably only by Friday."

"That's not too bad… our flight's in the morning, so hopefully we'll be up and away before the storm hits."

"Yeah—he said to make darn sure that we're on that plane."

"Thank goodness we have reserved seats," I said, "so I can still get to see my clients tomorrow and Thursday."

"And I'm going to schedule bull sessions with the staff today, and leave tomorrow for final executive meetings."

Leon and I didn't cross paths until that evening, although I did notice him in the lobby briefly while I waited for a client. We had agreed to meet with Mitchell at the same eclectic coffee-shop and bar where we had met the previous day.

Mitchell was in a much better mood. The installation of the new air conditioners was proceeding well, and provision had been made to place the remaining AC units in the foyer of the main building until the hurricane had departed.

"With a little luck, we'll all be finished with our individual responsibilities by tomorrow evening," I said.

Mitchell was more circumspect. "Not sure about that…. I'm really pushing my men, but they'll probably be able to do the rest without me." He looked every bit the worried executive.

"Whatever happens, let's get together to celebrate our accomplishments tomorrow evening." I looked at Leon, who was more familiar with Curacao than Mitchell or me. "Where are you going to take us that can top the restaurant on the cliff?"

Leon looked at me with a sparkle in his eyes. "*Trust me* — I know just the place. But remember to bring your biggest piggy bank with you. This place isn't cheap."

Thursday came quickly. During the course of the morning, I was able to see six existing clients, one after the other, starting with a married couple who joined me for breakfast. Later, my junior suite came in handy; while one client was with me, my next client was waiting to join me while sitting in the lobby. No sooner did I complete business with one, than the next one came to me for consultation. It worked almost like clockwork.

I barely had time to breathe. Lunchtime was spent in the company of an important client. I had brought him a bottle of a very expensive cognac in appreciation of his referring two new clients to me. The afternoon was spent in similar fashion. Sensing that I was running late for my evening get-together with my two friends, I called Leon, who assured me that he would make the necessary 'adjustment' with Mitchell as well as the restaurant.

He was sympathetic. "Sounds like you're *knackered*. I'll reset our reservations for nine o'clock. That okay?"

I did a quick calculation. That would give me time to grab an hour or so of sleep, possibly more. "Sounds good."

While I was with my next-to-last client, the suite phone jangled. It was Leon, telling me that the best he could do, and *that* only because he was a good customer to the restaurant, was to get a reserved table for eight-thirty.

I made the mental calculation. "That'll be fine."

"So I'll see you in the lobby at eight sharp."

Pressure.... I guess we need some to challenge us to muster our emotions and summon our best abilities, to overcome obstacles, to rise to the occasion. Once the last client left my suite, with a final handshake and my assurances that all would be well, I took a deep breath and slumped into an easy chair. I called the front desk about the latest information on the hurricane, and was told that the first affects would be felt on the island 'probably mid-morning.'

I jumped into the shower, and took care of my ablutions. Putting on a new shirt, pants and jacket helped me recover from my trying day. I was happy with the results, but was in urgent need of some down time. I was looking forward to a pleasant meal and some animated chatter with my two travel buddies.

Leon was waiting for me in the hotel lobby. We immediately set off to Punda to pick Mitchell up. Once accomplished, Leon directed to cab across the island toward the village of Santa Catarina. "Where are you taking us for dinner?" Mitchell asked.

"There's a restaurant there, on the other side of the island, in a converted lighthouse, which has probably the tastiest cuisine on Curacao, bar none. Thought it would be a fitting send-off for the three of us jovial travelers. We should be there right on time."

We drove across dry scrubland, almost devoid of trees, with barely visible little barren rocky hillocks on either side of the narrow, paved road. We passed through the little fishing village on the wild coast, with colorful small sturdy fishing boats pulled up on the thin strip of beach, their fishing nets strung on drying lines flapping nearby.

I noticed that the wind had picked up quite considerably; the movement of the stubby trees and the laundry on clothes lines reflected that. There were very few people visible; the streets and bleak white-washed houses were totally dark.

"Hmmm. Should have taken that into account," Leon pronounced. "This is the exposed north-eastern edge of the island—the windward side. And out *there* is the approaching storm. In Willemstad the wind's not so brisk—at least, not yet. The town's more sheltered than over here."

The cabbie announced that we had arrived at our destination. All was dark, but opposite the cab's headlights we saw the dim lights emanating from a tall white lighthouse, with a tiny single-story house attached to it.

"Candle light," I pronounced.

"Something's wrong with the electricity," Leon muttered. "This whole area's usually well-lit."

The cab driver drove up the incline and approached the light-house carefully across the rocky, sandy terrain. In the distance, underneath a darkened and lowering sky, the wind-swept white-capped waves crashed loudly on the rock-strewn coast down below.

We saw a man hurrying out to greet us carrying a flickering hurricane lamp which lit up his features.

"Ah, that's Erich. He and his business partner Rosa are the owners of the lighthouse restaurant."

"Good evening, good sirs." Erich spoke in Dutch-accented English; he struggled with the lamp. A gust of wind waved it wildly in his hand. "We have a problem tonight: as you can see, we have no electricity."

Leon carefully put his head out of the window, narrowing his eyes against the blustering wind. "What's going on, Erich?"

"Ah, Leon… my dear friend, we'll have to postpone your dinner until the next time. Whenever the wind picks up, our frail system kicks off. We sent our other diners back to their homes and hotels about half an hour ago."

"Too bad, Erich. My regards to Rosa—was looking forward to your excellent food and beverages, and being served by her."

The cab driver took us back into town. Leon remembered another restaurant in Otrabanda, on the other side of the harbor. The three of us ate and drank, toasting our successful trip until well into the night. We would have stayed longer except for punctilious Mitchell reminding us that we had a morning flight back to Miami, if the oncoming storm permitted.

Just before we left the restaurant, Leon called his meteorological friend and asked about the hurricane. He reported the uncertain news to us. "It's going to be nip and tuck. The 'cane's coming directly at Curacao. It's going to be a Cat One direct hit—at least it hasn't strengthened… *yet*. I asked my buddy about wind speed, and when it's unsafe for a jet to take off."

"What did he say?"

Leon scowled. "He said that it depends where the wind is blowing from. He said that the runways here are east—west. Then he covered for himself: he said that *go—no-go* depends on various factors. If there's a crosswind of more than forty mph, *that* can cause problems. Then tailwinds and gusts can *also* cause problems. The width of the runway—*and its length*—can cause problems.... Gentlemen, *we* may have a problem."

Our cab dropped Mitchell at his bed-and-breakfast, and then Leon and I retired to our individual rooms at the hotel. The following morning, I awoke to a 'the morning after the night before' walloping headache. I showered, shaved and packed my suitcase and roll-on.

Downstairs, I had a light breakfast in the dining room. Leon sidled into the chair opposite me. He looked as bad as I felt.

"Mornin'," he growled. "Where's the coffee? I don't feel so good. Must be the booze, or maybe the stress. My meteorological pal says that American and Avianca aren't coming in—too dangerous, they say. Our plane is already there, on the runway. But the air traffic controllers are still undecided about whether to abort or allow take-off."

My headache thrummed. Painfully, with eyes half-closed, I observed, "We'd better be off to the airport. There's always hope. Remember, this is the last flight to Miami until the hurricane passes by."

We got safely to the airport; the cabbie drove very carefully, aware of the blowing gusts. The wind was whipping up, and I had a sinking feeling that the flight would be called off. Mitchell was nowhere to be seen, but other hopeful passengers were milling around.

We checked in, hoping that all would be well.

"Hell," Leon said. "This is going to be a memorable trip. We either come home on time, or we remain holed up stranded in a luxury hotel on a strange tropical island."

In spite of my incapacitating headache, I put up a brave front. "Let's go through baggage and passport inspection *now*. I'd like to check out what they have in Duty Free; I promised my daughter to bring her a souvenir from Curacao. I'd also like some of that delicious Curacao liqueur."

Leon said that he'd join me; he had some gifts to buy as well.

Sometime later, we had purchased what we wanted to take home. We wandered out to the departure terminal. We were astonished by what we saw. There, on the runway, its jet engines in full pre-take-off throttle, was a plane, the only plane still at the threatened airport.

Suddenly it lurched forward, its jets shaking as it started its takeoff down the runway.

"Hey, that must be our plane!" Leon protested loudly. "Why didn't they announce it?"

"What the hell? We didn't hear any announcement!" I howled angrily.

"Sorry," the gate agent said, "but the P.A. system had problems. And the window for take-off was very short."

"That's not our fault," I explained angrily. "We had seats on that plane!" Suddenly my headache overwhelmed me.

"Don't worry — I'll take you."

Leon and I wheeled around to examine who was speaking. We saw a pilot, his elbow casually propped on a raised bar, captain's epaulets on the shoulders of his white shirt, and a broad smile on his lips.

I was incredulous. I looked at the empty runway, then back at the pilot. "How? D'you have a trained seagull out there to fly us on?"

He smiled confidently. "Come here and let me show you my 'bird.'"

Incredulously, we approached the observation window. There, tucked into a corner, looking for all the world so very small and inconspicuous, was a tiny airplane.

"It's a six-seater. And since you're passengers of our Netherlands Antilles Airlines, I can take you to your plane."

I laughed out loud. "You'll take us to our plane? And to Miami as well?"

He shrugged, smiling. "Your plane to Miami is presently on its way to *Aruba*, to our west. It will be there for about forty minutes, loading and unloading passengers and baggage. If we take off right now, we can catch it. I've got clearance to take off."

Leon and I were inside the little six-seater lickety-split. We were joined by a woman and her mother who had also missed the boarding announcement.

My headache mysteriously dissipated. We took off into the stiff wind, circled around and flew over the western part of the island. Soon it was behind us. We flew just above the choppy sea; the churning white-caps appeared to be very close. The pilot told us that he was instructed to fly lower than usual—at less than two thousand feet—because of prevailing weather conditions.

We were peering forward between the pilot and copilot. Suddenly in the far distance an island appeared. "That's Aruba," said the pilot.

In another few minutes we had taxied to a stop right under the overarching wing of our Miami-bound plane. Thanking the pilots profusely, gratefully, Leon and I hopped aboard and claimed our seats.

Mitchell looked at us wide-eyed as if we were visitors from another planet. "Where were you guys? I almost got thrown off the plane, I protested so hard that we were taking off without you."

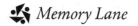

"We wanted to extend our visit to the last possible minute," I said, my eyes sparkling. "We were almost stranded in a foreign land."

❧

Note: Hurricane Joan roared through Bonaire, Curacao and Aruba, causing damage to structures and disruptions in electricity and water supplies. It then strengthened in the Caribbean Sea to a Category 4 storm, causing widespread death and destruction in several countries in Central America.

3

Feuding Neighbors

*T*he Jerusalem border between the Hashemite Kingdom of
Jordan and the State of Israel was one of the most tightly
guarded political frontiers on earth. The fractured city was split
asunder by a meandering demarcation line which was originally
drawn as a hastily-prepared cease-fire line between the warring
sides at the conclusion of Israel's War of Independence in 1948.

The Arab States—all seventeen of them at the time—vehe-
mently rejected the United Nations resolution to allow the Jews
in mandatory Palestine to declare the independence of a Jewish
State in a small section of the British mandate. Four Arab armies,
abetted by three others, invaded the fragmented fledgling nation.

The Jews, utilizing every available means and against all predic-
tions, were able to expand out of their splintered allocation and
increased the territory originally assigned to them. They fought
valiantly to get to Jerusalem, which incredibly wasn't part of

their intended allotment. A Jewish State without its holy city and historic capital? *Inconceivable!*

Once the United Nations was finally able to convince the warring parties to agree to a cease-fire, they sent officers and observers to arrange a contentious separation, not only in Jerusalem, but also in the area-at-large.

Unlike most borders separating countries, the border, especially around Jerusalem, paid no heed to logic, and no attention to the need for the safety of the city's residents. No consideration was given to topographical obstacles as it cut willy-nilly between the contending forces; the thin demarcation line between the two sides was brutal in its illogical geographic incision.

Whole neighborhoods were cut in half, arteries were cruelly dissected. Sometimes one side of a street was in one country, the other side in another. The demarcation rolled down ravines and across hills, separating one part from the other. To add to the confusion, some areas were designated as "no man's land," neither in Israel nor in Jordan.

The zig-zigging mess was crowned by an even bigger absurdity: Mount Scopus was left as an island of Israeli territory, an *exclave,* completely surrounded by the Jordanian section of eastern Jerusalem. Access to this tiny piece of Israel was severely restricted; the U.N. cease-fire agreement only permitted Israel to send a twice-monthly convoy of heavily reinforced buses up to Scopus to relieve the 'policemen' who guarded the grounds of Hadassah Hospital and the campus of the historic Hebrew University, now suddenly rendered useless, abandoned and lifeless.

My tank brigade—temporarily without its tanks—was pulled into Jerusalem to guard the Jerusalem border as a reward for eleven months of border duty in the desert opposite Egyptian forces in the south, in the central and eastern areas opposite Jordan or on the northern borders with Syria and Lebanon. This border duty was occasionally relieved by desert tank maneuvers to keep us sharp and battle-ready.

We looked forward to the assignment; the ancient city was world-class, with restaurants, coffee shops, book stores, movies and clubs to while away our time in during our off-duty hours. There was also the enticing possibility of meeting girls, something we only encountered during our periodic short visits home.

As I told some friends on the kibbutz which had been my home before being conscripted,

"Every time someone on the other side of the border *pisses* or *spits*, our brigade is called into action." My visits home were few and sporadic.

We and Jordan were confirmed feuding neighbors; we tried as best we could to be civil to them, while they hated and despised

us back. There existed only a tenuous cease-fire between us; a peace agreement was still decades away. Once every several days, and sometimes more frequently than that, someone from the Jordanian side of the border would open fire on someone on the Israeli side. Usually it involved a burst of bullets or an artillery shell fired out of hatred, exasperation or boredom, frequently by a lone red-*kaffiya'd* Arab Legionnaire.

This happened elsewhere as well, not just in Jerusalem. The Tel Aviv—Jerusalem railroad line, during its circuitous path through the forested and terraced Judean Hills, ran along the border for several kilometers no more than a couple of hundred yards from Jordan. In the early days of Statehood, Jordanian soldiers and villagers close to the rail line would frequently fire at the passing trains. Passengers were advised to lay low in that stretch of the journey. When Israel complained, the U.N. would issue a mild rebuke to the Jordanians. The matter was quickly resolved when the Israeli army acquired some mortars, which lobbed shells into the guilty villages; the Jordanians got the message.

The Arab Legion had been British Army-trained, but even in a disciplined squad there were hot-headed, undisciplined soldiers. Our response to the shootings had to be measured. It would have been madness to return fire in such a tinder-box, with large civilian populations on both sides of the zig-zag border.

Emotions ran very high in the city. The first time that our brigade came in to take over the border watch, I was put in charge of a border strong-point or emplacement. I was one of only a handful of officers who took turns with his men in taking guard duty. Although I was somewhat inconvenienced by this, it engendered solidarity and oneness among my charges. In the month that we guarded the border, no one was ever late to his assigned guard-time.

We and Jordan had existed side-by-side, but there was absolutely no connection between us. We might as well have been on two separate planets. *No* mail service; *no* telephone connection; *no* transportation links; *no* communication of any kind, other than grainy Arab TV and some radio broadcasts which were State-sponsored.

There was just one provisional access route between our two countries: the world-famous Mandelbaum Gate, which made it possible for certain carefully screened tourists and Arab residents of Israel to travel from Israel to Jordan and back. Some carefully-screened tourists who had been in Jordan were also permitted entry into Israel.

But these privileges came with definite limitations and restrictions. Jews were barred from entry, and Christian or Muslim tourists were required to carry *two* passports, their regular passport and a blank one.

The Jordanian border officers would not allow anyone to cross over who had any Israeli stamp in their passport. Even Israeli Arabs had to carry a 'stateless' blank U.N. passport with them to cross over.

The emplacement I was put in charge of was a two-story solidly constructed house with access to the flat roof where we stood guard; it was right on the border, with a similar emplacement in Jordan directly opposite but slightly lower, down a slight decline.

The distance between us was not much more than twenty yards. Our roof had a little reinforced sandbag-and-concrete bunker-like structure at the edge, facing the enemy. This little bunker had a narrow door in back, and contained a small stool, a field telephone and a pair of binoculars. There was a tiny rectangular vision and firing slit in the front wall. The Jordanian emplacement had something similar, facing us. The field telephone in our bunker was the cranking kind; a swift couple of hand cranks put the caller in touch with headquarters.

Our primary responsibility was to observe the seven border houses opposite us, including the Jordanian emplacement, and the area behind them, which included a gently sloping hill dropping down to a valley; on the right-hand side we could see a large village, just outside of Jerusalem.

The two emplacements were separated by a chest-high concertina wire entanglement delineating the international border between them; an occasional pole kept the wire in place. The houses strung out along the border were a minor aggravation. We had to shout—in Arabic, of course—at the kids who strayed too close to the barbed wire. And there was a house, four houses away from us, whose balcony jutted out just far enough to be in 'no man's land'; whenever we saw house occupants on the porch, we chased them inside. (The width of 'no man's land' varied from just a few yards to a wide swath in less-built-up areas.)

Our secondary responsibility was to observe and report all military traffic coming and going on the Jerusalem—Jericho and Jerusalem—Bethlehem roads, which we could see on the slope of the Mount of Olives to our left. We would observe the military traffic through field binoculars, and relay their division insignia and numbers to headquarters.

Downstairs was a large room with cots and mattresses for my soldiers. I had my own tiny bedroom, furnished with a cot, mattress and tiny night table. A bare low-wattage lightbulb provided illumination. We also had a toilet and small kitchen, with a cold-water sink and single hotplate: very basic. All we could do in the kitchen was to boil water for coffee using an ancient, blackened copper *finjan*.

Three times a day I would send my men, three or four at a time, carrying their mess-tins, through a small pine tree wooded area, down a well-worn path between some scattered houses, to a

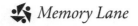

clearing where a field kitchen would be waiting. Rain or shine, this mobile field kitchen serviced us and two other nearby emplacements and then went on to other locations. Immediately behind our emplacement, on the far side of the little pine tree copse, there was a three-story nurses' training school and dormitory. The Israeli nurses were a constant distraction for the Jordanian soldiers, especially in the mornings and after their classes; they would chat excitedly amongst themselves on the long porches which ran the full length of the building's upper floors. We could see the Legionnaires using field binoculars to stare at those wild and carefree modern Israeli young women, so very different from their own. To our deep regret, the building was partially hidden from us by the pine tree woods.

❧

I first 'met' my opposite number in Jordan on the day of the fire. A brush fire had begun down in the little valley to the right of our position. I was alerted to the fire by one of my guards stationed on the roof; I clambered up to observe. The fire was advancing methodically through the dry grass and small bushes, throwing off a lot of smoke as it moved toward the wider area of 'no man's land,' helped by a stiff breeze.

I noticed a tall Arab Legionnaire officer standing on the opposite roof surrounded by regular red-*kaffiya'd* soldiers. He was giving orders, waving his arms; I could see soldiers scurrying to do his bidding. Six soldiers scampered out of their emplacement and took out their collapsible battle spades which came with their British Army-issued gear.

The Legionnaire troops started digging into the sparse rocky hill, intending to throw the dirt onto the fire. To the hilarious delight of some onlookers behind us on the Israeli side of the border, including the nurses observing from their porches, the dirt they found was being blown right back into their faces and eyes. Suddenly there was a massive explosion, which rocked my guard and me sideways. One of the 'fire-fighters' put down his shovel and grabbed his rifle, pointing it at the nurses. A magazine swiftly kicked into place. He fired two sharp rounds, drowning out the sound of the crackling fire. My guard and I were momentarily frozen in place. The other Arab Legionnaires had also dropped into firing positions.

I looked over at the tall Legionnaire officer on the roof. He raised both arms skyward and shrugged. I pointed at his soldiers and yelled—in English: *"Order them to stop! We're not firing at your men. That was an unexploded mine in 'no man's land' which blew up!"*

The giggling banter from the nurse's school had changed into cries of panic. I dispatched one of my guards to go and see what damage the two bullets had caused.

Suddenly, there was another large explosion from the area to my right; the blast again shook the ground. I flinched and automatically crouched down, pulling my guard down with me. A quick glance over to my adversary showed that he too had flattened himself on his roof.

The explosion came from where the flames had entered a section of 'no man's land.' To my dismay, the six Jordanian soldiers started firing at innocent civilian onlookers on the Israeli side. I could hear the shots, as well as the reload.

I again yelled, with more urgency, across the twenty yards or so separating us. "*Get them back inside your emplacement! We're not firing at them! Those were explosions from 'no man's land.' Get them back inside before they start a war!*"

The Jordanian officer raised himself up and looked over at his soldiers, more than a hundred yards from their emplacement. He barked guttural instructions. His soldiers got up and shouldered their rifles; they warily watched the fire, which by now had entered deep into 'no man's land,' the flames fueled by tinder-dry brush and assisted by the brisk breeze.

I scrambled into our little reinforced 'bunker' and contacted headquarters. They had already been notified about the mysterious explosions. I explained that I was in touch with my opposite number on the Jordanian side, and had persuaded him to get his Legionnaires to cease firing. I watched as single file, they began nimbly jogging back toward their emplacement.

Just then additional explosions occurred. Shells, bullets and projectiles began flying in every direction. It was like a crazed fireworks display gone awry. I understood that the explosions were caused by stray munitions and personnel mines which had been carelessly left behind or dropped at various times during Israel's confrontations with its feuding neighbor.

My soldier returned from checking on possible civilian casualties; an ambulance had been called because one of the nurses had been lightly wounded by a ricocheting bullet. I relayed that information forward as well. A colonel at headquarters wanted my assessment of the situation. I told him that things were tense, but a military confrontation, a cross-border conflagration, had been avoided. He wanted to know what was causing the background noise he heard.

"It's just ordnance, sir. Unexploded munitions accumulated from previous engagements. Shells, mines and bullets are exploding and flying in every direction. A trainee nurse was lightly wounded on her left arm; she's going to the hospital by ambulance."

"Good. What about the Jordanian emplacement—are they quiet?"

"Things have quietened down, sir." I looked over at the Jordanian officer peering out of his bunker, every so often quickly vanishing inside when there was a particularly heavy explosion.

"Can you talk to him, let him know that we don't want a cross-border exchange any more than he does."

"I've already done that, sir."

"*Ahh.* Okay."

The late-afternoon sun shone through the smoke still swirling around the fire and the locations of the explosions, gradually dissipating in the brisk breeze.

The Legionnaire officer was standing on the edge of his roof, looking in my direction. "*Nice evening,*" he said. "*All quiet now.*"

I approached the edge of my roof. "*Yes. Really silly for people to die over a brush fire. Better that we find a way of living in peace.*"

He nodded solemnly. A small victory.

The next morning, I got a call from my uncle, a New York surgeon who was visiting Israel at the time. He had contacted me through my brigade's phone number; they were able to patch him through. He had no idea that I was in Jerusalem.

"Glad I reached you," he said. "Where are you? Can we get together? By the way, I just heard that there was a border incident in Jerusalem yesterday."

"Yeah, I know. It wasn't a big deal", I said matter-of-factly. "I'm here—in Jerusalem.... I was involved in that little border skirmish."

4

Her Secret

*A*ll of the following happened a very long time ago, when life was less complex, and the future had no horizons. The world seemed to spin effortlessly on its axis, and my first real girlfriend and I were young, and in love—the carefree, I-just-can't-believe-this-is-actually-happening-to-me kind of youthful, exuberant love.

We had felt our way forward, moving smoothly from our first encounters to getting to know one another as we navigated carefully through the potentially turbulent and perilous straits of growing familiarity. Eventually, excited and full of youthful anticipation and hopefulness, we experienced the awe and delight of sexual intimacy.

The decision to move in together came easily; the prospects were endlessly appealing. This, we both exclaimed breathlessly and sincerely, was going to be an exhilarating mutual experience which would add meaning to both of our lives.

We carefully chose our apartment, selecting a cozy one-bedroom on an upper floor with a great view of the spread of the city below. The mutual decision to go shopping for the things we needed to fill our love-nest followed naturally.

The sofa we eventually purchased was large and el-shaped. The colors, I thought silently at the time, were not those I would have chosen. In fact, it also didn't fit into the elevator, nor the stairwell. Young love and brilliant insight presented a 'thinking out of the box' solution.

We resolved the problem by winching the sofa up from the ground, guiding it from the roof, then pulling and maneuvering it carefully through the porch sliding doors and into the apartment.

That sofa, and the challenge it presented, took on a significance of its own in its couple-hood symbolism. Its acquisition had been a big deal for us; it was the largest and bulkiest object we owned, other than an aging aluminum-winged automobile.

Before deciding on the sofa, I had been accustomed, as a single man-about-town, to acquire my own furniture, all of it preowned. At that time, I hadn't thought too much about matching styles or even colors. As long as the item filled a need, I would find a way of buying it.

Once she and I began dating, things had, in very subtle ways, begun to change. I discovered that my former uneven and unstable dating landscape had been deeply plowed into unfamiliar furrows of commitment. Before her, dating hadn't really brought about any real change in my outlook or attitude.

Early on, she and I both realized that our growing bond was meaningful. Nonetheless, I was surprised by the speed in which she had captured my heart; our union had quickly developed apace.

Things glided along beautifully; when we decided to live together, she had begun asserting her wishes and tastes. I was totally smitten for the first time in my life; I had given her the green light of my consent.

Once we were in our own little love-nest, we copulated lovingly and lustfully. We did it whenever we wanted to; late at night, in the early morning, sometimes a 'quickie' before showering prior to going to work, and then again upon arriving home. The eager urges were mutually shared and enjoyed.

During those first months of blissful cohabitation I had been ecstatic with the wonder of her body, which I possessed happily, and she mine. As my one true love, my willing partner in the thrill of our adventure, she was my sexual equal. Not only our bodies but our minds were fused in the thrill of sharing our lives. But, imperceptibly at first, the uniqueness of our relationship began to slowly lose its gloss. My guess was that we grew to accept our mutuality and began to take it for granted.

The first time the subject of my sexual preferences had come up, our L-shaped sofa played an important role as backdrop. I had gotten up and had paced the length of our living room and back again, explaining, and hoping that she would see what I wanted from her.

She had sat against one arm of our cherished sofa, her arms thrown around her legs, her head propped on top of her knees. She had listened silently, searching for the right response. Sitting there at the time, her hair spilling onto her breasts, she had appeared so vulnerable, so small and defenseless, that I had to quash my impulse to bound over and comfort her, and reassure her of my undying love. But I restrained myself; I wanted an answer to my question.

"Why can't we do this thing together, you and I?" I pleaded. "It's important to me. I need to feel that I can express sexuality in any way with you, just like a lot of other couples do. I love you— I want us to share this."

She had hesitated, staring at a slowly-moving point of light through the window. "It's not that I'm against it…. It's just hard for me to explain." She nodded slowly, as if affirming the veracity of her explanation.

Again, I felt the urge to take her in my arms and tell her that it didn't matter, that I loved her just the way she was. But my cussed immaturity directed me to persist in my quest.

"Listen," I said quietly, against the distant thrum of traffic. "This is something we have to work around. I need you to understand that we can do anything we want to, together. Just anything that you and I decide on doing."

"I get that, but can we discuss this some other time?" She looked away from me, looking at the same point of light as before. She gulped; I thought that she stifled an urge to sob.

I took her in my arms, reassuring her that we'd be able to smooth things out. After all, we loved one another. Looking down at her, I saw once again how beautiful she was, and yet at the same time how very vulnerable.

A while later, lying in bed after ardent lovemaking, I had raised the issue once again.

"Is it something you're opposed to because of some religious or moral reason, or something? I mean, when couples get together sexually, most anything goes. That is, if they both want it."

She cut me off quickly. "No, I don't think that it's a bad thing."

"So why the reluctance on your part?" She took her time responding, measuring her words. "I'm not quite there yet. Please ... give me a little more time."

The very next occasion that the topic of sex came up, she sensed that I was starting to take her reluctance as a personal rejection.

"Listen, my love... I don't know where we're going with this.... Do I turn you on?" I asked, as we were getting ready for bed. She probably thought that I was bewildered, almost boyish in my obvious exasperation.

"No... no! Please don't get the wrong vibes, sweetie. This isn't about you... I love everything about you. It's just something I have to work through. Something not related to us, I promise."

I imagined that she could see the anguished hurt deep inside my eyes.

"Please... believe me, honey. This has absolutely nothing to do with you. It's something... something that I have to work out for myself. You... are *wonderful*.... I'm very attracted to you... I want you to know that."

She was playing a precarious balancing game, in which things could swiftly end up out of kilter. She sensed she was beginning to lose me, in spite of all her fervent assurances.

The following day she felt a perceived distance between us, something that she intuited had not been there before. It wasn't anything I said, or did, but the effortless ease of our bond was now beginning to falter, almost struggle. Clouds were now hiding the lovers' moon.

That night in bed she tried to reassure me once again. We then tossed about with abandon in our lovemaking. After our passionate writhing was over, I pulled her close. In the pitch darkness, we faced each other, nose-to-nose. I sensed her pert and willing face;

her body contoured mine. "Sweetie, did you have a bad experience once?" I whispered, knowing that my words, so very softly spoken, would resound in her ears. She lay there, hardly breathing. Persisting, I delved deeper.

"You didn't want to do it at that time, but you did it anyway?" My words hung in the air above our heads like a lifeless silken flag awaiting a breeze.

She didn't utter a word, but she noticed an imperceptible movement on my part, as if her silence had been an affirmation which had finally sunk through. I moved right up against her ear, touching it with my lips, as if to be at one with her brain, connecting directly to her inner being, without any constraints.

My words reverberated deep inside her. "Did someone force you… did someone once do something you didn't want?"

So very close to her, I was fully aware of her slight affirmative nod by the mutual movement of our heads.

"At some friggin' frat party or other?" I whispered, trying to comprehend her anguish.

"No… it was much… earlier." she intoned, her words passing into the ether.

Finally I caught on. "How old were you when this happened?" She had pushed back into the protection of the bed, remembering the panic and the pain of her encounter. "*Eight*…I was just eight."

I slid my arms around her shoulders, protecting her as best I could from the memory of her trauma. Wordlessly, we lay there, listening to the mutual beating of our hearts, at one in body and soul.

5

Old Houses

O sbert Hawkins had built the rough-hewn hunting lodge on land which he and his brother Titus had inherited from their father.

Eventually, at the urging of his wife Ann, he had started to build a small Tudor country home next to it. She had pointed out to him that she and their two children would enjoy the country air and the space to run and play, to explore and be in touch with nature. The house they owned in town, in Tunbridge Wells, in an expensive neighborhood, was somewhat cramped, with a small garden in front and in back

Osbert was well established in Tunbridge Wells, owning a drapery, material and cloth shop in a fashionable area of town. Ten years before, rotund and balding, he had married well. Although a confirmed bachelor, he had become entranced by Ann, eldest daughter of Cecil and Margaret Rowland, among the town's elite. He had wooed her and won her heart. Their engagement party was celebrated on Michaelmas Day, a symbolic portend of fruit-fulness, and were married in June of the following year amid all the pomp and splendor that the occasion demanded. Two children followed in short order: Edward and three years later, Joan.

Osbert's family were Roman Catholics. As with all of his co-religionists, and indeed by all of England, he had endured many years of fluctuating fortunes, depending upon which monarch ruled at any given time. The period was marked by alternating outbursts of mayhem and murder, and the feverish hunting down of clergymen and aristocrats, both Catholic as well as converts to the newly created Church of England alike. The Catholic monarch murdered upstart Protestants; Protestant rulers zealously liquidated Papists.

A prosperous merchant and a man of stature in the community, Osbert had initially decided to build the hunting lodge to add some enjoyment to his life; grouse, pheasants, partridges, wild boar and deer were plentiful in the area.

He fondly remembered the enjoyable times he had spent in his youth hunting with his father. He had found hunting to be a suitable diversion to his regular mundane avocation of purchasing and handling different bolts of cloth while catering to the fabric needs of his mostly landed gentry clientele.

Through a contact in London, he had recently introduced intricate Reticella bobbin lace from Belgium, which became much sought-after in the town; society women competed with one another for the most elaborate designs for the edging of their clothing. Imported lace tablecloths were also considered a measure of one's social standing, the larger and the more elaborate the better.

Growing up, Osbert had always been closer to his father than his younger brother Titus; he had tried to emulate him, to use him as an exemplar on how to conduct his life. As a youngster, he was rambunctious and adventurous. Titus was his exact opposite: he was introverted and studious. Their mother influenced Titus' future with her devout religiosity: she took him to church, sometimes three times a week. He would endlessly gaze at the highest reaches of the cathedral apse as if he were searching for a way through to discovering the most intimate recesses of secrets untold. He also was able to repeat the prayers of the day in Latin, as well as the prayers of the Rosary and the Eucharist.

Their parents died within a year of each other, his father from pleurisy, his mother succumbed to consumption.

It was thought at the time that the area's chalybeate (iron-heavy) spring water wasn't as healthy as some had thought. But there was also substantial steel and iron mining and smelting in the area.

Osbert recalled that at a young age—it must have been when he was five or six, and his brother a year younger—his father had taken them hunting. Titus was never really into hunting with a bow and arrows; he gave it a half-hearted try, and his results were disappointing. But Osbert reveled in his father's attention and encouragement.

"Remember, Osbert," his father had said, "first assume a solid shooting position. You cannot shoot accurately if your feet are not solidly grounded in the right posture. Next, *nock* the arrow, like this." His father had once again demonstrated how the arrow is nocked in the bow. "Next, draw and anchor the bow. Then aim: your right hand flexes, so that the tip of your nose is right on the string…. Remember to flex your back and leg muscles; that makes your arrow fly true. Then release the string in one fluid motion, and follow through."

His father had proudly observed Osbert do it, following his instructions. "That's it!" he had said delightedly, when Osbert had hit an assigned target. A short while later, Osbert had bagged his first grouse, and then, immediately after, had killed his first wild boar. His father had roared with delight.

Once he committed to building his country home, to Ann's absolute joy, Osbert Hawkins was advised by his father-in-law Cecil Rowland to employ Master Builder Nicholas Hopewell of London to design and build his new home.

"Nicholas Hopewell is one of the finest designer-builders around. You and Ann will be very content with the results," he had said over dinner one evening.

Osbert had leaned back and wiped his mouth with his serviette. "Do you think that he would come out here to take a look at my plot and come up with a proposal?"

Cecil Rowlands was a wealthy man with substantial knowledge about buildings and land in general. He had invested heavily in a new shopping street in Tonbridge, about four miles from his palatial home.

"I don't see why not," he said, guiding a forkful of venison into his mouth. He masticated for a minute, swallowed and continued. "This is what you should do, to get Hopewell to commit. First, you'll travel to London with a rough sketch of the plot. Remember to include all the specifics you mentioned to me about your property: of course, the dimensions and the topography. Take with you all the details about available building material in the area, especially around Mayfield—that's where your brother is a priest, correct? Hopewell will want to know where he can buy local timber, good quality timber, and straw, plenty of it. And brick: we have a good supply around these parts.... Also the availability of skilled workers—masons, tilers, carpenters, thatchers and plasterers." Cecil Rowland reached out for his wine glass, turning away while his palm came into contact with the rim. He gently tinkled his ring against the glass, deep in thought. "And don't forget about where he can get wattle and good sources of clay. Then he'll probably take a day or two to calculate the costs, including his time in traveling. Remember, it'll take a full day to get from London to Mayfield. Then you'll find a way of getting him to—what? *Five Ashes*, right, where your land is? He may well assign most of the work to a couple of his assistants. Don't worry—they're very competent. And Hopewell will be at your bidding, always."

Hopewell was duly engaged. Once the builder showed him his proposed design plans, Osbert Hawkins realized what a fine house it would be. The plans called for timber frames, wattle, mud and clay daub plasterwork, brickwork, high chimneys and ornate hearths. There were batches of mullioned windows, with shallow oriels on the second floor and tall gables along the roof line.

Inside, the builder incorporated finishes in specialized rooms for study, dining and sleeping; finishes included linen-fold paneling and plaster-relief ceilings. He used Osbert Hawkins' easy access to cloth and tapestries in order to partition rooms. He utilized molded strapwork to create symmetrical geometric patterns on the outer walls.

Hopewell, always the innovator, also introduced glass-paned windows, unusual at the time. Local labor was employed. Hopewell's construction supervisors had temporarily taken up residence in the nearby village of Mayfield; the house was being completed quickly and efficiently. The builder himself came down from London a couple of times to observe the progress.

Always prompt and orderly, Osbert started going to his hunting lodge every second Saturday, leaving around midday, doing some hunting, staying at the lodge overnight, hunting again in the early morning, and returning home by Sunday's gloaming. He preferred sleeping in his lodge, rather than in the nearby nearly-completed structure, but he did spend some time in the house, just sitting in a corner of a room, visualizing what it would be like to live there.

On yet another visit to his brother Father Titus, Osbert made him an offer. "Ann loves the new house. She's so intent on getting ahead, of being a leader in her social circle, setting a trend. Our house will encourage others to buy property out in the countryside." Osbert laughed out loud. "But methinks she has a point. Our plot there on the ridge would even be large enough for a full-sized mansion with extensive gardens, not just a house and a hunting lodge. If you want a share in the house as it is, Titus, because the land is half yours, I cannot deny you that."

Titus demurred, but with a dangled condition. "I'm just a humble priest… but who knows what the future holds, now that England is under Elizabeth's sway…. When King Henry ruled, once he forced his marriage to that hussy Ann Boleyn, he made life intolerable for us Catholics, especially priests, and that continued under young Edward—"

"*Aye*—and then things returned to normal under our good queen Mary. It's such a pity she died so quickly -"

Father Titus leaned closer to his brother Osbert. "We may yet have to pay dearly for Mary's excesses. So many Protestants perished during her reign… including here in Mayfield. I knew a couple of them personally, the ones who were burnt at the stake. We were all good practicing Catholics until damn Henry dragged England away from the Pope, illegally, of course, because our Pope denied the annulment of Henry's marriage to good queen Catherine of Aragon."

"Yes, and then Henry declared that he was the Supreme Head of his new church. What gall!"

Father Titus nodded. "Henry and damned Archbishop Cranmer built a case that our monasteries and churches were centers of vice and corruption, and that they were treasonously plotting against the Crown…. At that time, that was all a figment of their imagination. It was all *concocted*: all we wanted was a return to the old order."

Osbert clucked and snapped his fingers, frowning. "I thought for a while that the northern revolts against Henry would succeed. But Henry was wily like a fox. He took control of the monasteries, and sold them and their lands to loyalists in the provinces. So the revolts petered out." Titus cupped his two hands. "And now we're back in the hunt. But this time once again, we're the hunted." He subtly indicated a certain unrest; Osbert picked up the hint, and the two brothers hugged. Osbert got on his horse and rode toward his town home.

Osbert continued to ride out to his hunting lodge, usually alone. Occasionally, if he left the lodge early enough, he would ride into Mayfield on his way home after Titus finished Mass and ecclesiastic duties in his parish church. Mayfield was a small country town about two miles from his hunting lodge in the hamlet of Five Ashes, and about ten miles from his town home.

Osbert made several visits to the new house, sometimes accompanied by Ann and their two children. Ann was delighted with the larger rooms and the quality of the construction. Osbert smiled as he watched the fruits of his investment taking shape, and saw how happy Ann was. Their children Edward and Joan took the measure of the estate, exploring all of it, including the woods and the meadows, and then running down the hill to the narrow lane, stopping to throw stones into a small lake at the edge of the property.

Tired and happy, Osbert, Ann and the children slowly rode home in the family wagon.

When the time came to interview applicants for the positions of housekeeper, cook and gardener, Titus helped, because

Osbert and Ann wanted local candidates for those positions. Titus announced the available positions by word of mouth, and there were many applicants. Ultimately the couple selected their staff, and traveled with them to the new house.

On another weekend trip by himself, he exchanged greetings with the occasional pedestrian travelers and horseback riders, reaching the country town of Mayfield by two of the clock; he heard the church tower strike the time. He found the door shut, whereas usually the rectory door was open for congregants to come and go as they pleased. *This is a sign of the times*, he thought. *Churches and rectories were never shut in the good old days....*

Once the house was complete, Osbert, Ann and their two children stayed there for one full week. It was idyllic; the children helped the gardener plant shrubs and flowers in the bare front garden. Ann busied herself with chores inside and out. Some furniture arrived in one cart, and then another. She requested seeds for a vegetable garden; the gardener laid out the boundaries.

They entertained Titus for dinner on a couple of occasions. The children really liked their newfound freedom to wander and explore.

Once the family returned to town, Osbert continued to come to the lodge; he regularly came to the new house while he was there, but preferred to sleep in the lodge.

On a late-summer day, Osbert was on his way to his hunting lodge. The day was pleasant, and he sat astride his chestnut gelding enjoying the ride down the narrow lane. He fondly touched his new bow, picked up from a bowyer on the previous day; he had testing its tensile strength, and found it to his liking. At the same time, a couple of shops away, he had shown an interest in the newest innovation, the hunting gun. He had handled it, looked down its length, examined it carefully, but then had decided against purchasing it. "It would be unduly cruel to the animals, shooting them with a gun," he told the gunsmith.

Afterwards, thinking about the conversation, he realized that he should consider the new hunting gun in the future, since he believed on reflection that there was more chance of injuring and maiming the animal with a badly-placed arrow than with an iron ball.

He passed a few farmers who were taking their merchandise to market; a toothless farmer carrying a yolk on his skinny shoulders, with six cackling upside-down chickens hanging from each arm; a farmer laboriously pushing a handcart with a bad wheel, upon which he had precariously placed four rough jute sacks of garden vegetables; an older man and a younger (his son?) struggling to carry a long bloody board, covered by a jute sack over what appeared to be the carcass of an animal. Osbert Hawkins was inquisitive "Pray tell, what manner of animal lies underneath yon sack?"

The older man, panting from his effort, stopped momentarily, causing the younger man to run up against the end of the board. "Mi'lud, 'tis a fine fat porker, salted an' ready for the pot, spit or pit."

At a signal from the older man, they placed the board on the grassy, stony side of the lane, pulling the coarse jute sack off to reveal the pig.

Osbert Hawkins admired the plump hog, assuring himself that in a short while he himself would be able to bag a similar animal.

"*Aye*, 'tis very fine — ye'll have no problem selling that hog, handsome as it is."

He continued on his way, guided by the winding lane as it picked its path between hedgerows, stacked rock fences and plowed fields. There were very view sign-posts along the meandering, narrow lane. More than once, he had taken a wrong turn, causing him to have to retrace his path. Eventually arriving at the hunting lodge, with the prominent new Tudor house rising on the highest ridge, Osbert went out hunting. He knew of an excellent area for grouse and partridge hunting, on the bank of a fast-flowing stream.

Arriving at the river bank on horseback, he trod carefully, his bow ready in the meaty part of his holding hand; the arrow was nocked securely, ready to shoot. Suddenly, a flush of grouse rose out of the reeds, drumming and thumping loudly. As they flapped away, Osbert recovered his poise, positioned his feet, checked the nock of his arrow, drew his bow, arched his back and released.

"Got it!" He quickly pulled another arrow from his quiver, aimed quickly and saw another grouse fall a distance away. A short while later, further up the river bank, he added a third. By the time he got back to the lodge, it was getting dark. He lit the fireplace with kindling wood, and put the wild boar, two pheasants and five grouse inside.

The following day, he inspected the progress of his house on the ridge. He left three grouse for the staff, By midday, he had loaded up his horse with the rest of his hunting spoils. He set of for his brother's rectory, hoping that by this time that he would have concluded the *Sext* prayer at noon. He took two plump grouse with him as a gift to his brother, hoping that he wouldn't dirty the rectory with their blood.

Osbert found the door once again locked, an indication of the religious tension in the country at large. When a Catholic monarch ruled England, Titus could keep the doors to his rectory and the nearby church wide open; with Elizabeth now ruling, things were fraught with danger. Osbert explained through the heavy shut door that he was Father Titus' brother. A peep-hole to the side opened, and he was examined. An acolyte ushered him in; he presented the grouse to a servant. He found Titus in his study, praying with an older priest, unknown to Osbert.

Eventually, Titus glanced up and acknowledged him, signaling him to enter, proffering a chair.

"Sorry to interrupt you."

Titus ignored the apology with a swipe of his hand. "God's work is never done. The good Lord will permit us in grace to continue at another time…. Monsignor Erasmus, this is my brother Osbert, from Tunbridge Wells. The good Father's on a mission…"

Monsignor Erasmus interjected quickly. "On my way to Hastings, actually. Began my trip in London. Your brother has kindly invited me to spend a couple of days in the rectory. My horse is tired and my cart's wheels need repairing."

Titus bade Osbert to sit; he sat opposite the priests.

"I've just come from the building site," Osbert began. "Things are progressing fast. So fast that I'm almost temporarily running out of money -"

Titus interrupted. "My brother's building that house I was telling you about, Monsignor. It's not too far from here. It's a *real* possibility -"

Osbert was intrigued. "Possibility for *what,* Titus?"

Titus and Monsignor Erasmus spoke simultaneously, looked at each other, then bowed diffidently. Titus took over the conversation. "Osbert, there's a very real possibility that our lives hang in the balance."

It was 1590; Elizabeth I had initially consolidated her power and had refrained from aggressively persecuting Catholics, but that had suddenly changed. England was in religious upheaval once again. Over the years, several Catholic plots had been uncovered to depose her, and Catholic clergymen were being hunted down, captured and summarily executed as traitors. Osbert was confused. "Do you think that these purges will affect us here as well? And if so, what has my new house got to do with this?"

Monsignor Erasmus sighed. "Your brother Father Titus and I are planning for the eventuality of having to hide large numbers of priests and religious artifacts in out-of-the-way places, where Elizabeth's zealous priest hunters can't reach them. Our faith is under attack, and it's going to get a lot worse, so I've been told by those who know about these things in Elizabeth's court."

Monsignor Erasmus and Father Titus exchanged a quick glance, and the monsignor nodded.

Titus addressed his brother. "Osbert, we need your help… urgently."

"What's wrong?" Osbert was confused and concerned about his brother's appeal.

Titus observed his brother intently. "This is a matter of the utmost importance. I need you to understand what is happening to our devout Roman Catholic clergy. The Protestants are now exacting revenge for the terrible things we did to their Protestant reformer clergy, to some of their aristocrats, and even to some regular citizens. Our former queen Mary, may the good Lord show her extreme grace, mercy and compassion, tried to eradicate the upstart new faith, branches of which have sprung up throughout Europe as well. I can only hope that we can overcome the insanity before a bloodbath occurs."

"Amen", said Osbert seriously. "And what exactly can we do about all this bloodletting?"

Father Titus leaned forward, his face reflecting the gravity of what he was about to say. "Listen, dear brother. You and I own that plot of land where you've built your country home. Monsignor Erasmus and I have discussed this; I want you to build a larger house there, with our help. We have access to the necessary funds. This house will serve as a secret hiding place for our priests, not only from this area of Sussex and Kent, but, if Heaven and the good Lord grant us our wish, from all of southeastern England. What say you?"

Osbert was astonished. "How ... I want to help, but... How am I going to build this... this house... on our property? I don't -"

Father Titus instinctively knew what his brother's objections would be. He had thought out not only his own logic, but also the potential objections his brother could raise.

"Listen, brother... listen carefully. As I said, we have money, and Monsignor Erasmus will donate still more. We can build a larger house, add to it. The secret is to build places for our worthy priests in out-of-the-way places in order to be safely hidden. I have two priests who before they became men of God were skilled in carpentry and bricklaying and plasterwork. They say that it can be done."

Osbert wasn't ready to concede: not yet. "I already have an excellent builder in Master Nicholas Hopewell, who built my house in the first place."

Tutis shook his head. "It's not a good idea—Master Hopewell under threat of his life may reveal certain secrets about the house -"

"But he's a good practicing Catholic—I happen to know that."

Titus was adamant. "Osbert—this is a top-secret mission. The rebuilding should be done by our two craftsmen. The secret of what will be done, and where the priests' hiding places will be, will be safe in their hands."

Osbert was still caught up in the viability of the effort. "If they— the priests—are found out, our lives are in peril as well. Ann, and the children would be—"

Titus was not to be denied. "Of course. That's why we have to make their hiding places *impossible to find*. Elizabeth's zealous priest hunters are after our priests in all the likely places because they have refused to take her 'Oath of Supremacy.' Their lives are in great danger."

Osbert opened his mouth to make a rejoinder, but Titus interjected. "Time, dear brother is of the essence. Think well on these matters, and come back here tomorrow, at the noon hour, rain or shine. I'll have the two priests here who can do this for us. Now go home and rest. My salutations and my blessings to Ann and your children. And tell her that she won't regret the changes we make to her house."

The following day, Osbert entered Titus' study at noon. He saw four pairs of eyes — priests' eyes — looking at him. His brother arose, then Monsignor Erasmus, and then the other two.

Titus shook Osbert's hand, and put out an open hand in the direction of the others. "Osbert, Monsignor Erasmus you already know. He's here in an advisory capacity. These are the two men, both humble *men of God*, who will do the Lord's work for us, protecting our priests from harm. Father Anselm and Father John — those are their names now."

The two men introduced themselves; Father Anselm was the brick and plaster-layer; he was the older of the two. Tall and skinny, he looked as if he had endured hard times; there was a haunted look in his eyes. Father John was quiet and shorter in stature; he was a master carpenter, who like Father Anselm, has found his calling in the church later in life.

Father Anselm looked first at Father Titus, then at Osbert. He summarized what they wanted to do, depending on the construction. "There's so much that can be done to disguise, distract and spirit away. When a search party arrives, looking for our folk, speed of concealment is vital. At the same time, we have to consider the possibility of escape. We can incorporate secret passageways, even tunnels, leading through the foundations of the house and out, through an orchard, or copse of trees. "Father John and I will first consider immediate hiding places, secure enough that even close observation won't reveal them. But first of all we must have your permission -" he looked again at Osbert "-before we do anything. So let's have a look at your Tudor home. Then we can have a better idea about what's to be done."

Father Titus sent an acolyte down the High Street to a farmer who was a parishioner. He came back riding a long flatbed cart, sitting behind two farm horses. The group set off to look at the house.

Once there, the two priests in charge of construction walked around the house, knocking on the outer daub caulking and some of the outer wooden beams. Osbert followed behind them, wondering what the house would look like once the builder-priests were finished, and whether Ann would approve.

Inside, they quickly grew excited about the central staircase, and muttered about having plenty of room for pilasters and false walls in certain rooms. They were enthused about crawl space and the area around existing hearths and wainscoting. The three chimneys and the possibilities of the attic and roof spaces brought looks of excitement in their eyes.

Sensing Osbert's confusion, Father Anselm began explaining what exactly they planned to accomplish. "You'll be happy with the results. It'll be an elegant brick building on the outside. with protruding windows, rows of three in front and in back. Two stories, utilizing burnt clay overlapping tiles on the roof. Inside, we're not going to make structural changes, apart from the stair-case, the fireplaces and the chimneys. We'll build some pilaster columns around the house, some of which will be false.… We will also build a couple of secret escape passageways connecting to an escape tunnel or two. We know of several absolutely reli-able local tradesfolk who can help us do everything I mentioned."

They reported back to Monsignor Erasmus and Father Titus.

Father Anselm's eyes reflected his excitement in meeting the challenge; his tormented face had become invigorated by the solutions and the hope engendered by the house. "If we build an outer brick wall and make some additions and improvements, this house could easily house thirty or more priests-in-hiding. We also would have ample space to store vestments and altar furni-ture. We could provide for space where Catholic services could be held in complete safety and seclusion. I mentioned that we have several excellent tradesfolk who know what we want to achieve. All we need are a few more reliable workers, and of course sufficient money."

"We can find the necessary labor among our flock at the church," said Father Titus. "They are loyal and hardworking, and once the work is complete, they'll return to their former employment, and no one will be any the wiser." He looked at Osbert. "Brother, you have to approve the changes. Once we are out of these religious wars, hopefully soon, you and Ann will have your larger house for your use, for sure. And we have the funds to construct it."

Titus looked at the two builder-priests." Brothers-in-faith, my brother has the final say in whether we do this or not. All I can hope is that we can achieve our objective: to build a safe-house in this out-of-the-way place for our brother priests. If my brother indulges us, may the good Lord in His infinite mercy bless our work and our life-saving mission."

His horse was thoroughly lathered and foaming; he sensed the borrowed horse had reached the end of its tether. He had reached the outskirts of Tonbridge. He saw the dimly lit alehouse he was familiar with, the 'Dragon and Shield.' He dismounted hastily, and looked around: no-one had followed him.

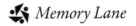
Good—I have some time, but I can't rest yet. How very stupid of me to be embroiled in the foolhardy attempt to blow up the Houses of Parliament! Did I really believe that it would be so simple to achieve? I got enthused because this looked like the best way to end the persecution of Catholics, by killing as many important Protestants as possible, including King James himself. What a fool I was—we're all going to pay for this with our lives, if they catch us.

It was 1605, fifteen eventful years after Osbert Hawkins had committed to expanding his country home. He and his wife Ann were now the proud parents of four children. Their eldest son Edward was now helping his father run two cloth shops: the original one in Tunbridge Wells, and a branch in Tonbridge. Pretty Joan was now betrothed: a decision was to be made about where the secret Catholic service would be held when the time came for nuptials.

The religious wars in England had become a lengthy reign of terror. After Elizabeth's death in 1603, James VI of Scotland became James I of England, and the persecution of Catholics continued unabated.

Several uprisings had been crushed. The Catholics were desperate. They continued to plot revenge. A group of plotters recruited a certain Guido ('Guy') Fawkes, an English convert to Catholicism who was so fervent about his new faith that he fought for ten years in the army of Catholic Spain while they battled unsuccessfully to quell a Protestant revolt in the Netherlands.

He became an expert in explosives.

When the plotters came up with their plot to pulverize the English Houses of Parliament (and reduce to rubble a large part of central London as well), Guy Fawkes was their man. He will forevermore be memorialized as the man who was guarding thirty six barrels of gunpowder in the basement of Parliament when he was discovered. Those that know say that someone among the plotters sent a letter warning someone important not to attend the opening of Parliament; on such insignificant things hinged the fate of a nation.

Father Anselm tied his bone-weary and thoroughly drained horse to a stump, and waddled unsteadily into the alehouse, his legs trembling uncontrollably. He spied a familiar figure, that of Percy Gainford the tavernkeeper. "Greetings, Percy. I need a favor of you—a really big favor."

Percy Gainford peered into Father Anselm's sweat-streaked face, his brow lined with worry, a deeply haunted and exhausted look in his eyes. "Greetings, Father Anselm. I see that you've come from afar, and in a great hurry."

"Aye, that I have. And a mite more to travel — I must to … to Mayfield this very night. *I can't tell him exactly where I'm going. That would be injudicious and dangerous.*

The tavernkeeper took stock of Father Anselm. *He's obviously in great haste. Is someone chasing him?* "What are you asking me for? A horse, perhaps?

"Yes, Percy. I'll pay you handsomely for a good, sound horse. Mine is hobbled and exhausted, right outside. Please take good care of her. I drove her hard, all the way from London."

"London, eh? What's going on there?

I can't tell him anything. Best to say that I'd been called back to Mayfield for a parishioner. "A parishioner is in dire straits — I've been called to his bedside for last rites."

The tavernkeeper closed one eye, and leered mischievously at the priest. "*Father Anselm* — we've known each other for a very long time. There are some things spoken truthfully, but some people, even priests like you, will tell untruths to confuse us, using your Godly connection to cloud the revelation. I'm not one t' be confused or paltered to."

The priest weighed his options; the innkeeper was persistent. "Percy, things may pass my lips that would cause harm to innocents. I cannot say…. But I need a good steed to get me to Mayfield, quickly."

"Aye, right you are. Follow me." The tavernkeeper led an exhausted priest to the back of the tavern. A figure loomed in front of them. "Greetings, Master Percy," the figure said quietly.

"Thomas, my stableman," said the tavernkeeper by way of explanation. "I'm taking Betsy out for day or two.... Father Anselm, follow me."

It was dark, pitch black, but he knew where the saddle was, hefted it and clucked several times at the unseen horse which nickered softly. In the dark, Father Anselm heard Percy pat the horse, talk to it, and then heard something slide across the horse's back. The tavernkeeper grunted and attended to the horse. In pitch blackness, he smoothly slid the headstall on, and clucking encouragement once again, led the horse out into the courtyard.

"She's a palfrey, a good horse, goes by the name of Betsy. Take good care of her. I want her back in a day or two. Only to Mayfield, hear?"

"Of course, brother Percy. Of course," the priest said, greatly relieved.

"Now, because we've known each other for a long time, and I want my place in Heaven assured, I'm going to charge you just a Groat for my beauty here, plus an added deposit of an Angel." Percy shrugged in the semi-darkness. "Have to cover for eventualities, you know, even though I know you to be an honest man, and a priest, to boot."

Father Anselm nodded, and reached into his cassock, turning his back on the tavernkeeper. He counted out the coins. "How much for taking care of my poor horse out front?" he asked, clinking the coins in his hand.

"Let's have a look at her…. *Thomas*, I have another horse out front that will need some attention. Follow me."

In the dim light coming from the tavern, Thomas and Father Anselm stood by while Percy carefully ran his practiced hands up and down the exhausted horse, its head down, in desperate need of water and nourishment.

"Your horse, Father?"

"No, Percy. I *borrowed* her in great haste, may Heaven and the good Lord forgive me."

Percy grunted. "Thomas, take her to the stable. Give her her strength back. Take good care of her until Father Anselm here comes back for her…. That'll be another Half-a-Crown for boarding her."

Father Anselm galloped away, anxious to reach his rectory. In the dark, he had great difficulty in keeping on the narrow lane once he left Tonbridge, with just an occasional light to guide him.

If they're coming after me, and I know they will, they'll leave it to daytime to chase me down.

His backside and legs ached; the solid wood seat underneath the thin leather skirt chafed his rear. *Just another few miles, and I'll be half-safe. Tomorrow I'll complete my disappearance. How utterly foolish of me!*

He reached the rectory in the very early morning. Nothing stirred. He took Betsy into his stable, and fell soundly asleep.

The light of dawn awakened him. He walked over to a parishioner's home, swore him to secrecy by invoking all the dreadful nether-worldly things that would occur if he ever revealed where he would be hiding, explaining that it was a matter of life and death. Then he told the parishioner where to return Betsy, and requested a cart ride to Osbert Hawkins' house in Five Ashes. He paid handsomely for the favors, even though the parishioner professed that he was ready to do his bidding for nothing.

Within an hour, Father Anselm had disappeared. Two days later, a search party turned up at Osbert's and Ann's house, determined to find any and all Recusants, then torture them and put them to death; another diligent search of the house three weeks later also came up empty.

Guy Fawkes was tortured. He revealed the names of all the other plotters, many of whom had left London, fleeing to their provincial homes. The great majority of them were found guilty, hanged, and then drawn and quartered. Fawkes, on his way to the gallows, jumped down and broke his neck. His head was displayed on a spike as a warning to the general population of London.

🍂

I was just eleven years old, living with an uncle and aunt who six months earlier I had met for the very first time. A whole series of family tragedies in South Africa had forced me to relocate to England, since my uncle and another uncle in the States were my last surviving blood relatives.

It was the beginning of the summer break from school. My aunt had decided that she and my uncle plus their son would be going on holiday to Dinard, on the north coast of France. I wasn't included in their plans; I didn't mind at all. Still, I was apprehensive and yet somewhat hopeful about where I was now headed. I was being transported to the cavernous, bustling Charing Cross Station in London by my uncle's van driver.

At least I won't be seeing my aunt Frieda for the next six weeks.... She makes it obvious that I'm not wanted in the family, her family. I'm relieved that I won't be going with them. She convinced my Uncle George to find some other holiday venue for me, while they and my cousin go away on their annual holiday.

I was in the passenger seat of my uncle's van as it moved through the busy city traffic. The driver, Bert, tried to make polite conversation with me.

"So you're off to Tunbridge Wells, eh? To some kind of a camp, right?"

"Yes. My uncle found this school for me. Actually right now it's a summer camp for boys. And then tomorrow my uncle and aunt and their son go off to France."

"Do you mind going off by yourself, then?"

I thought for a long moment. *I think that I can trust him.* "No, actually I'm looking forward to not being with them for a few weeks. But I don't know what kind of a place I'm going to."

Bert was sympathetic. "I'm sure you'll find it to your liking. Probably lots of boys from all over will be there. Should be fun."

We arrived at the busy station. Bert stopped the van and retrieved my suitcase from the back. A London Bobby was already briskly signaling for him to depart. "'ere you go, then. D'you know how to buy your ticket, and where you're going?"

"Yes. To Tunbridge Wells, and then I wait for someone from the school to pick me up. I'll be all right."

Almost three hours later, the open-top car deposited me on the gravel driveway outside an imposing two-story building. The driver, who told me that he was Captain Bucknall, the Headmaster's son, waved toward the front door.

"Go inside. In Reception, you'll find Mrs. Darling—she'll take care of you."

I entered, looking to the left and right as I proceeded down the wainscotted corridor; the walls were filled with black-and-white framed photographs of the school's cricket teams; all the players were in cricket whites, the last batsmen still wearing their batting pads.

I found the 'Reception' door, and entered.

Mrs. Darling was expecting me. She relieved me of my suitcase, saying that someone would take it to the lockers.

"Are all your clothes labeled?" she asked. "Good. I suggest you remove any books and personal items now. You'll find a night table next to your bed in the dorm. I'll ask Mr. Spours to take you over there. You'll be in Braithwaite. Bucky sleeps there too."

Noticing my bewildered look, she smiled. "Oh, I know it's a little confusing. Braithwaite is our largest dorm, with twenty eight beds in it, with night-stands for each for your personal things, like books. Mr. Harold Bucknall, or 'Bucky' as we all call him, is our Headmaster. He sleeps in Braithwaite where the large bay window is, which overlooks our swimming pool and sport-fields.

"You'll like it, I'm sure…. Oh, here's Mr. Spours now. He's our cricket coach…. Mr. Spours, could you take Henry here to Braithwaite?"

Mr. Spours, a tall and rangy man in an open neck shirt, slacks and sports jacket, smiled. "First time here? Oh, then you deserve the full tour. We'll stop to pick up another camper, who came just a few minutes before you…. Henry, eh? Where're you from, Henry? Watford, huh? I have a cousin who lives nearby, in Bushey…. D'you play cricket? Good, then you'll be able to hone your skills with us…."

We passed through a series of connecting corridors, arriving at a door with a sign on it, saying "Tavistock."

"This is one of our regular dorms—usually eight to ten beds in them." Mr. Spours knocked and entered in one motion. "Ah, Errol? Say hello to Henry, from Watford, Herts. And you're from? Oh, London, eh? And originally? Ah, from India. That's good, that's good. Lots of our students during the school year are from that part of the world. Come with us, Errol, you're going to get the full newcomer's tour…. Let's start in the front of the building." He looked at Henry. "Oh, first I'll take you to Braithwaite, so that you can stow those books and personal items by your bed."

We two campers followed Mr. Spours through the twisting inner corridor; we followed it until we reached the front door.

"This is a *really* historic building. Do you see that brick wall? Well, there used to be *another* wall inside it, made of exposed timbers and beams, with whitewashed wattle-and-clay in between them. They had a dickens of a job removing it. In the early 1600s, hunted priests used to hide between the walls…. "Bucky—Mr. Bucknall, our Headmaster, told us that when he bought the building right before the Second World War they had to almost completely destroy the inner wall during renovations. What a mess!

"Anyway, when they were getting close to tearing all the old wall down, the Royal National Historic Society got wind of what was going on here. There was such a hue and cry that a special Act of Parliament prevented any further demolition. You can still see the old Tudor wall in several places around the building. The study and the music room upstairs still have the old wall inside, as does the kitchen and storeroom, the way it was back in the 1590s."

Mr. Spours looked at Errol and me. "Who's the mathematician here? *Henry*, how old is this building? It's now 1950...." I had already done the calculation in my head. "*Err* -Three hundred and sixty years old, more-or-less." Mr. Spours looked at me, satisfied. "That's right—it's *old*... very old.... Are any of you Roman Catholic?—*Never mind*, I shouldn't have asked. "But the Catholics—*especially* the priests—were terribly persecuted back when Elizabeth was queen. Thorough searches were made in this very house to find '*Recusants*'—that's what they called anyone who didn't take Elizabeth's 'Oath of Supremacy.' Any priest who didn't was accused of high treason, and *murdered*, once they found him. "Let me take you to the Library," he said, excitedly. "I have something special to show you."

We walked back toward the Library. "The Libe, as a generation of our graduates has called it, has always had a reputation of being eerie, or creepy—here it is."

He opened the door, and was surprised to see someone inside, other than the librarian. "Hello, Bucky! What a surprise!" Mr. Spours turned to the two of us. "This is Mr. Bucknall, boys—Mr. Bucknall is our Headmaster—"

'Bucky' crinkled his eyes; they slitted with mirth and genuine pleasure. "'*Bucky*' to you, boys—everybody calls me 'Bucky' sooner or later: you might as well get used to it."

'Bucky' was slightly stooped, wore small eyeglasses and had a quiet but assured demeanor. The two of us and 'Bucky' exchanged greetings. "So what's Mr. Spours been telling you about this old building?

"That it's full of surprises," volunteered Errol.

"True—and he brought you to the Libe to show you the secret passage, correct, Mr. Spours?"

"Why, yes, Bucky. Do you have time to talk to us about it?"

Bucky looked around, and smiled. "Why not? Boys, there's a history around this passageway. Remember that this house, which has been called Skippers Hill Manor for at least a couple of hundred years, was used as a hiding place by Catholic priests during the religious wars in the late 1500s and the early 1600s."

Bucky looked at the two of us, smiling in an avuncular manner. "So young sirs, do you know anything about Guy Fawkes' Day?" "Certainly, sir" I said, confidently. "That it commemorates the Gunpowder Plot to blow up the Houses of Parliament in London."

"Excellent, young man. It should actually be called 'Guy Fawkes' *Night*,' because that's the night that we spend tens of millions of pounds to explode fireworks and crackers and send rockets bursting into the night sky.

"Well, all that happened in 1605, during James I's reign. One of the plotters to blow up Parliament was one Father Anselm, a local man who was the priest concealment genius who reconstructed this very house. "When all those barrels of gunpowder were discovered in the basement of Parliament, most of the plotters were rounded up fairly quickly. The unfortunate Mr. Guy Fawkes was guarding the barrels, since he had experience with explosives. They imprisoned him right away, and tortured him for information.

"Father Anselm was deeply involved in the plot, and fled London as quickly as a horse would take him. He left a trail, which the priest hunters followed, all the way back to Skippers Hill Manor, this house. He had built some wonderful hiding places here; they never found him. Over the many years, there were persistent rumors that he had also built an escape passage somewhere in this manor, but no one had ever actually found the entrance.

"But," his eyes sparkled as he raised a pointed finger, "back in 1946, we installed some new shelving in this very library." Bucky looked around, his eyes slitted with mirth. "Well, someone must have stacked too many heavy books on the upper shelves, and one of the heavy bookcases came crashing over, smashing the wainscoting over here." He walked over and pointed.

"Behind the wainscoting, we saw a deep hole, a crawl space. I was called over. The librarians enlarged the entrance hole, and I sent one of the younger teachers into the passageway to have a look. He was a smaller fellow, lithe and very athletic. He came back after fifteen or so minutes, and told us that the passageway had side connecting passageways, and eventually led to a tunnel outside of the manor. If a priest needed to escape completely, he could have gained access by means of the connecting passageways, but I'm not at liberty to tell you where they are." Bucky smiled an apologetic smile. "Suffice it to say we have them all blocked and boarded up: we can't have our young men traipsing around in secret tunnels at all hours of the day and night."

Mr. Spours showed his appreciation. "That's a wonderful insight, Bucky."

Bucky laughed. "I thought so myself. I see myself as the connection between the original builders of this magnificent old manor and modern times."

I also see myself as a validator and authenticator of that historic old house: after all, I was there for five summers in a row, and *loved* the experience. I didn't miss my uncle or my aunt at all—especially not my aunt—or my cousin. I was happy being away from them, in a place where I first discovered the earliest glimmers of myself as a worthy individual, after so much of my having been beaten down and diminished as a child.

Recently I've been in touch with the school on the internet. Through Google, I learned that Harold 'Bucky' Bucknall passed away in the early 'sixties. The ownership of his private school went to his son, Captain Bucknall, whom I met such a very long time ago, when I was an impressionable eleven years old. I never told him why I was so silent when he took me into town to catch the train back to my life with my draconian and harsh aunt; I was choking back tears of regret, regret at having to leave my haven of happiness. I was hated by my aunt; she relished making my life miserable.

❧

Students continued to come to Skippers Hill Manor Preparatory School for Boys from many parts of the world. Commonwealth countries, especially India, Pakistan and Ceylon (later Sri Lanka) were steady sources of student enrollment for young men in their early teens. That and local recruitment kept the school solvent until the nineteen eighties. At that time, less favorable student recruitment prospects obliged Captain Bucknall to sell out; an international education corporation became the new owners.

The old house is now four hundred thirty years old; I've only known her for the past seventy. We've grown older together. Now, in the late years of my life, I can only wonder about the old house's resilience and longevity, to which I bear witness. It has survived many modifications, and through the years, new annexes and portable classrooms were built around it. The house still graciously overlooks the quad, the swimming pool and the sports fields in the gentle slope down below.

At sunset, the woods and fields in the hushed and tranquil valley still further down glow with a timeless persistence which reminds us all that nature is deep and unfathomable.

In the manor, strange inexplicable noises are sometimes heard during the night by 'dormers'; a slight creaking sound, across floorboard to floorboard, as if someone is walking by, close, very close; something metaphysical, almost supernatural, hovers nearby in the diaphanous swirl. Students swear that during the night, on trips to the toilet, other-worldly spectral breezes brush by them, baffling and unexplainable.

Osbert Hawkins' ghost must still wander his house, so proud at having the means and the desire—obviously encouraged by his wife Ann—to build it. As he effortlessly wanders

the creaking corridors he definitely encounters the satisfied rambling ghosts of Father Anselm and Father John, who
fundamentally expanded the house in order to save so many
innocent lives.

There's also no question that Bucky's effervescent spirit is there
as well, silently checking on the latest crop of youngsters, smiling as he flits effortlessly, gliding, coasting, from dorm to dorm
in his old school house which he loved so much.

NOTES: I enjoyed the challenge of creating the rationale for the
building of the original Tudor house back in the 1590s. It was a
historic coup, an accomplishment, to write about those distress-
ing and intolerant times, when one wrong word, spoken carelessly,
could mean the difference between life and death.

I made one historic error in the story, but decided to leave it
uncorrected. I placed Osbert Hawkins and family in Tunbridge
Wells in the 1590s. I discovered while writing the story that that
city didn't come into being until the early 1600s. The reader will
hopefully forgive me for this inadvertent error, which doesn't
detract at all from the story-line.

6

On Becoming an Orphan
in an Exotic Land

*H*enry had hovered at the edge of that unfortunate black hole designated by humans as 'becoming and orphan' for a very long time. Once the giant trees of our protective familial circle start to tumble, the probability of becoming an orphan becomes more and still more likely.

Very early in his existence, while still a baby, Henry had suffered the tragic personal loss and terribly bad fate of losing his mother to thyroid cancer. His father Siegfried, pitifully ill-prepared for such a tragic reversal, cursed his luck and cast around for a surrogate mother. To this day, it's unclear how he overcame the loss of his wife and the mother to his baby boy. Possibly an agency for new immigrants in Cape Town, South Africa offered some assistance. He also had some cousins in Johannesburg; time has washed away any trace of how he raised little Henry for the first two years of his life.

I still miss my mother. I can only imagine, after seeing other doting mothers with their children, what I have missed by not having a mother in my life. I'll forever be grateful to my mother for giving me life, but I miss the loving, guiding—sometimes meddlesome, but well-intentioned—hand a mother wields throughout her life.

When little Henry was two years old, his grandparents—Siegfried's parents—arrived in Cape Town as refugees from war-torn Europe. They already had guarantees of housing and work in Johannesburg, a thousand miles away. To add to their absorption concerns, Siegfried must have prevailed over their weak objections and convinced them to take little Henry with them to Johannesburg. This arrangement was to occur several times during Henry's formative years, whenever his father couldn't care for him. As time and later circumstances would prove, he was not a very competent and involved caregiver.

I cannot imagine what my life would have been like without my doting grandparents. They both gave me the 'strokes'—the love and the reassurance—even when everything around me crumbled to clay.

Henry's father Siegfried had been a minor diplomat in Austria's consulate until Hitler seized power in March of 1938; after that, he reverted to playing the cello, which he had done profession-ally in Europe, all the while looking for an opportunity to find something more rewarding, more substantive.

Henry was somewhere around three years old when his father met an opera singer's daughter, possibly at a "Nights in Vienna" concert; Joy was already a divorcee in her early twenties when she married Siegfried. At that point he had brought Henry back from his grandparents, and the three of them moved into a big newly–constructed house in a Cape Town suburb while he started working as a cosmetics salesman. Henry remembers that one room of the house was filled with little aluminum containers of cosmetic powder.

This period of my life was full of promise unfulfilled. The semblance of apparent normality was just a façade.

Siegfried's luck eventually turned; Henry remembers an impor-tant meeting in a rich man's villa. While Joy and her stepson Henry walked in the beautifully-tended terraced gardens and sat next to the villa's swimming pool, Siegfried successfully negotiated with the millionaire, and was appointed Managing Director of an older sea-front hotel, just off Cape Town's famed ocean promenade.

Joy later gave birth to a daughter, Jeannie, and the four of them lived in a cramped suite in the hotel. After finding this arrangement unsatisfactory, the family moved to a villa outside of Cape Town, overlooking the ocean.

I was always looking for security: the feeling of being protected. I didn't fully realize it at the time: how could I? I was just an overly nervous kid. I began peeing in bed, that's how loud I was shouting. I felt deeply embarrassed, but it was involuntary: I couldn't control it.

Henry was a lonely boy. His early memories are of constantly being relocated, never in one place long enough to form friendships, always changing schools, neighborhoods and even cities. In Cape Town he liked to roam the rock pools on the sandy beaches, and explore the huge primordial rocks close to the shore, some of them with holes large enough to walk through standing up. This he did mostly by himself, rarely with friends. This 'aloneness' was to remain a part of Henry's character for the rest of his life.

People later called me 'aloof.' Although I emphatically deny this, because I'm capable of great warmth with those I know and love, those I feel comfortable around, there is definitely an aspect of my character which seeks solitude.

He missed his grandparents very much. He remembers 'writing' a letter to them, finding an envelope, and taking it to the mailbox. Although his father and stepmother observed him writing it, no one helped make sure that it arrived safely.

Siegfried and Joy settled into the routine of raising their two children. Outwardly, things seemed to be blissful. Siegfried was preoccupied with the hotel; staffing and housing the help were giving him problems. Joy spent her time raising little Jeannie and keeping an eye on Henry. He remembers going to one school, then being pulled out due to moving from near the center of the city to a suburb.

One day on the beach, he and a couple of new-found friends found a large Portuguese Man o' War. He found a discarded cigarette tin, and tried to scoop the jellyfish into it. Stupidly, he touched the tentacles and was badly stung; he tossed the tin away, and in great pain, walked home.

Always looking for interesting things to do, on one occasion while combing the beach he and another boy encountered an illusionist, who attracted a large audience. He amazed the crowd by escaping from handcuffs and from a locked sack. When the magician announced a further show at two p.m., he and his new-found friend made certain that they were back in time for the show.

Siegfried encountered continual staffing and employee housing problems; there was a constant battle to maintain current operating licenses. After every inspection, there were things which needed correcting, but no sooner was one citation corrected than another had sprung up. Joy was busy with her baby, as well as with Henry.

All supposedly was fine for a year or so. By age six, Henry was able to travel in by bus to the Saturday morning movies in downtown Cape Town; his father showed him how to do it just once, and Henry managed by himself after that. Henry's father had no compunctions about allowing his son — in fact, he encouraged him — to commute in by bus, as if this was safe and protected pre-war Vienna and not an exotic African location.

Looking back, Henry was amazed at how irresponsible and irrational his father was.

I have adult children of my own. Thinking back to the distant times of my childhood, I'm shocked — dumbfounded — that my father was so oblivious of the dangers engendered in permitting a six-or seven-year old to travel unaccompanied in to a big city. I absolutely wouldn't have allowed my own minor children to do this. One of my grandchildren is approaching the age when I was first introduced into travelling in to the city by bus; out of the question! No way!

On one occasion, in the dark of the movie house, Henry lost one of the two coins he needed in order to take the bus home. A search in the dim light at the conclusion of the movie failed to help in finding the missing coin. He noticed the box office outside the movie house. He stood in line, listening to what the people ahead of him were saying. Once it was his turn, he said, "one coin for two", or something to that effect. The cashier shook her head and said that she couldn't comply.

The bus conductor was also uncooperative; he let Henry out at a half-way point, and Henry walked the rest of the way home.

Many years later, on a visit to Cape Town, Henry retraced his forced walk, from the junction where he was let off, all the way to Camps Bay, where he once had lived; it was well over a mile, along a road which was hazardous and precarious for a small child.

I somehow accepted this as something I had to do in order to arrive home. I was lucky that things worked out well.

Henry celebrated his seventh birthday on the beach with a couple of friends from school, taking a hamper of food and soft drinks prepared by Joy.

A couple of months after his seventh birthday, he came back from his regular Saturday morning trip to the movies to find his father hunched over his desk, crying bitter tears. He asked his father what the problem was; apparently after a violent confrontation, Joy had taken little Jeannie with her, promising never to return.

The very next morning, Siegfried put his son on the train to Johannesburg, explaining that he couldn't accompany him, but that his grandparents would be at the train station the following afternoon to pick him up.

He remembers his panicky feelings of long ago, standing at the window of the train compartment looking down on his tall father who was standing on the platform. Ahead of him loomed an interminable journey in which he would be completely alone, 'for a day and a night,' as his father had said. This wasn't just a half-hour trip to the movies, which was scary enough for a six-or seven-year-old.

This was depraved, irrational behavior. I don't care how stressed my father was. He should never have expected this of me.

What happened the next day in both Cape Town and Johannesburg reveals the utter turmoil in Siegfried's life; he was a weak-willed man for whom playing the victim came easily. In large measure he brought about and caused the many calamities which beset him.

With a long whistle, the train slid out of Cape Town's central station. Henry sat down, frozen by his overwhelming lone-liness. A woman, a complete stranger, sat opposite him in the train compartment. After a while she asked him if he was trav-elling alone; he meekly admitted he was. She was considerate. She showed him where the toilet was. When mealtime came (*a porter walking down the corridor with a gong announced the meal in the dining car*) she explained that meals were included in the train fare. His father hadn't even told him that. She accompanied him to the dining car, and complimented him on his table manners. (*Living in a hotel had been a good preparation.*)

Had she not had the humanity and compassion to ask, no one would have been there to remind him where to go to urinate, or to go for a meal, or to bed him down for the night. It's true that he had been on overnight trips before, but they were always in the company of his father and more recently with his stepmother as well. And now his stepmother was no longer in the picture.

While he was in transit to Johannesburg, Joy had come back to Siegfried to leave little Jeannie in his charge; she disappeared thereafter. Both Henry and Jeannie were well on the way to becoming orphans, but there was much to unravel yet.

Over the years, Jeannie had been through a fate much worse than Henry's. She'd been deposited in an orphanage, and went through the trauma of being adopted, then returned to the orphanage, to later being adopted once again. Her father and mother had spurned her: what dreadful parents they were.

I met Jeannie late in life, after being separated for almost seventy years. She had no idea that she had an older brother until I began searching for her. Luckily for us, she had recently allowed access to her adoption agency records, which made it possible to contact her. She's a wonderful sister who was determined and resilient enough to overcome her childhood traumas. Subsequently she built a life for herself; she became a nurse, got married, and had two daughters, my late-found nieces.

For the next three-plus years, Henry lived with his grandparents. He settled into his grandparent's apartment, and found friends in the neighborhood, a suburb called Doornfontein. For the first time in his life there was stability and normality.

At the time Doornfontein was very Jewish. Many refugee and immigrant families settled there. He and his neighborhood friends went to the Jewish Government School, later known as King David.

His grandparents received a colored map of the State of Israel. How proud they were of that embryonic little country. Henry convinced them to let him borrow the map, which he wanted to take to school; he promised to return it. He lost it while in class.

He joined a Zionist youth group, and went on field trips with them. During the summers, he was sent to Jewish camps, hundreds of miles from Johannesburg.

He started a lifelong interest in sports; he remembers how South African national teams in Rugby and cricket competed with the best in the world. The first glimmers of being good enough to represent his school in team sports began in those years.

On Yom Kippur, Henry accompanied his grandfather to a fine old temple; it was the one time in the year that his grandfather attended services, following a habit he and Henry's grandmother had begun in Vienna, Austria.

Even though my wife insists that I'm religious, I've never been completely comfortable in a synagogue, especially an orthodox one. I'm much more culturally Jewish than being religious.

On New Year's Eve 1946, Henry's grandparents took him to a musical review. He got tired walking home after midnight, so his aged grandfather put him on his shoulders and carried him home.

Over the years, Siegfried had brought Joy and Henry to visit his parents several times. There was also a week-long trip to Pretoria, passing through Johannesburg (for what purpose Henry didn't know, possibly work-related).

Siegfried was visiting once again, this time because his father was hospitalized due to a heart attack. Everybody was putting on their winter coats getting ready to visit him in the hospital, when someone called from the hospital to announce that his father had died. Another tall tree and bulwark of Henry's life had been cut down.

After that brutal loss, Siegfried returned to Cape Town to wind up his affairs. To Henry's delight, his father had decided to come and be with his own mother and him.

Siegfried's life was in shambles. He lied to his mother that he was in touch with Joy. He said that his daughter Jeannie was with her, while in fact he had already handed Jeannie over to an orphanage for adoption while he was still in Cape Town.

Henry was once again sent to summer camp. At the time, Siegfried was working with his mother in an advertising company begun by his parents. They sold advertising on the four sides of the thick covers and the spines of telephone book binders. He was due back from summer camp in three days; it was December 31, 1947. Siegfried telephoned his mother and asked her to meet him at some downtown location. He must have watched her dutifully leave for the meeting from some locale close by her apartment.

He took advantage of her absence, and with Henry still away at camp, came into his mother's home; in great haste he put everything of value into some suitcases and fled. When Henry came back from camp three days later, his grandmother's apartment was still in a mess. Siegfried was gone forever from his son's life, and his daughter's in Cape Town as well. He was a despicable human being, slinking away and shirking his parental responsibilities. When his mother died two years later, he was nowhere to be seen.

I don't mean to pass judgement, but I absolutely have to. What kind of a father, what kind of a son, would do the heartless things he did? We all have done thoughtless things, terrible things in some cases. But my father's complete lack of essential heartfulness is indicative of a person devoid of compassion and of basic humanity.

Little Jeannie had become an orphan, dropped off and abandoned, later to be adopted, not aware that she had an older brother.

Henry spent the next two years full of fear, not fully accepting or understanding his tenuous situation. Like many small children existing in a deprived familial status or in a financially threatened condition, he never fully comprehended why he had become a latch-key kid; coming home from school to an empty apartment while his aged grandmother was working so hard to make ends meet.

His grandmother had accepted a position as a sales lady, first in a delicatessen, and later in a lamp-and lamp shade store. This burden was thrust on her, since she had a grandson to raise and bills to pay. She was already approaching her mid-sixties, and she was stout.

My poor devoted Ouma! She must have known that she was swimming against the current, that Death would finally overtake her. And still she went out every morning, whether she felt well or not, to make a little extra money to pay the bills and keep food on the table for the two of us.

Henry remembers getting some hand-me-downs: a used pair of sandals, a couple of shorts and some shirts. Like a lot of other kids elsewhere, he forced back his fears and hoped that things would turn out all right.

In December of 1949, he was once again sent to summer camp; all kids his age went to camp. The funds came from somewhere. Upon returning from camp, this time his Aunt Mania was at the station to pick him up and take him to her home. Henry suspected that something was wrong, but he didn't want to ask.

While she was bathing her own little boy, she remarked, "What a good *Ouma* she was", referring to Henry's grandmother. Her death was merely implied. Then, incredibly, she suggested that he go to his bedroom and lie down, to mourn the passing of his beloved grandmother. He dutifully went and laid down, but he was so frozen—actually *terrified*—that he didn't cry.

She was gone—buried in my absence. I never had the chance to say goodbye, to thank her for giving me a home, for taking care of me when my emotionless rolling-stone father couldn't. Many years later, I visited her grave for the first time: she'd been dead for sixty-seven years.

Henry was also now officially an orphan; his last remaining close relative, his beloved grandmother, was gone.

When does one become an orphan? When your parents die? Or is it when your last living blood relative, your last caregiver, passes away? Henry had experienced all there was to experience.

His Aunt Mania was in touch with Henry's uncles, informing them of their mother's death, and asking them whether they would be willing to receive Henry.

One of his two uncles—his fathers' brothers—lived near London. The other uncle lived in New York; both of them had harrowing experiences during the war years fleeing the Nazi scourge. They discussed who would take Henry in: Frank in New York was married, but had no children, whereas George in England was married and had a child. It was decided between them that he was to go to George in England, with Frank providing some financial support.

Henry celebrated his eleventh birthday in Parktown, at his Aunt Mania's spacious home. He invited a couple of his closest friends from his three–year sojourn in Doornfontein. He had mixed feelings about his trip to England, anticipation and apprehension tumbling through his mind.

Saying goodbye was difficult. In his heavy heart, he knew he was leaving his sheltered place, even though he had been dealt a cruel fate in losing his mother so early in his life, then losing his beloved grandfather, then his father's cowardly disappearance, and finally the one person who had been a loving and reliable constant in his short life, his grandmother.

The trip to Cape Town to catch the ship a week after his farewell birthday party was anticlimactic. Here he was, back in Cape Town, the city of his birth, less than a month after he had been there in camp.

His Aunt Mania had arranged for a friend to pick him up at the train station, and take him to the port. He saw the ship that was to take him to Southampton, England; it was the 21,000-ton *Durban Castle*.

I reflected on my fate. I was leaving my home, the country of my birth, the country that had offered succor and safety to my father, then to my mother, and then finally to my grandparents. I was just an 'accidental' South African, as my wife had told me many years later.

But there are three anthems—yes, three—that still today are very emotional. When I hear the national anthems of South Africa, Israel, and the United States, tears flood my eyes. They mean an awful lot to me, because my feelings are deeply invested in each of them.

I've been an orphan for a very long time, but these anthems remind me of the sense of purpose that all of us share as parts of our greater family, the family of Man.

7

Orphans

*T*heir neighbor rode up to the little house in a hurry. It was a raw day, with a brisk wind that brought flurries of snow with it. Shivering, he rapped hard on the door, until *Pani* Parenko answered. He quickly blurted the bad news, that her son and his wife had been killed by a landslide in the mountains while journeying between villages. Numb and paralyzed by the news, she hobbled heavily over to her tiny kitchen, sitting down with difficulty, her head in her gaunt hands.

What do I do now? My son, my poor son…. How am I going to take care of Tomas, not just for three or four days a week, but full-time? I can barely take care of myself….

She was bereft, but she no longer could cry; life had sucked her tear ducts dry and had hardened her heart.

She was a devout practitioner, a woman of faith. She hobbled to her bedroom and retrieved her Rosary. The beads ran through her fingers. On the crucifix, she made the sign of the cross and then started on the Apostles' Creed. She couldn't concentrate. To her amazement, a large tear streaked her right cheek; she hadn't cried for so long.

What better time to cry than over the death of my son and his wife?

She flitted through the Our Father, and then reached the first of the Hail Marys. She found that her mind was elsewhere. *Maybe I'll recite the Prayer for the Dead instead: that should do it.*

She petitioned God for the care of her departed loved ones. After a while, she came back to her awful reality.

She had let her grandson Tomas sleep while she busied herself with other pertinent matters. Several hours passed. Eventually, after speaking to a neighbor in muffled tones, she woke Tomas.

He slept in her tiny spare room, her sewing room, which she used as his bedroom; his grandmother had put in a bundle of clean rags, a puffy pillow and a blanket for him to sleep in during the many times that his parents travelled away from home. His father was a travelling minister, and his mother helped in preparing the sacrament and other arrangements for the congregants in several scattered villages throughout the area.

When Tomas appeared in the kitchen, still bleary-eyed, she had instructed him to sit down. She steeled herself for what she had to tell him.

"I don't know what to do, my dear boy." She limped unsteadily over to her favorite wooden chair covered by a soft cushion,

near the warming stove. In the flickering light, which emphasized her lined and wrinkled face, she sat down heavily, lean-
ing on her better leg to steady herself. She breathed laboriously,
wheezing.

"God only knows how long I still have to live…. Your dear
parents are no longer with us on this earth…. I just received
word that your father and mother… died… in a landslide some
distance away from town." Despite her difficulty in crying, her
eyes glistened.

"Our good neighbor was travelling by horse a short distance
behind them…he saw their cart and horse being swept out from
under them…. At this point, the neighbor said, it's not even
certain that their bodies will ever be recovered. They are… buried
underneath tons of earth, rock and downed trees. Understandably,
after telling me what happened, our neighbor hurried over to the
church down the street to thank God for sparing his life. He was
shaken to his core… another couple of minutes forward, and he
too would have perished.

"He's lucky—so lucky—that he had stopped to water his horse
by a stream, thus avoiding the landslide."

Tomas sat stoically, uncertain what to say, He was in shock,
having been awaked suddenly, but his emotions hadn't yet
coalesced after the trauma of hearing what had occurred to his
parents. Blinking hard, he was grappling with the terrifying new

reality. He sat and thought about what his grandmother would tell him. He feared that she would tell him that she was no longer capable of taking care of him, which she had done for several days at a time while his father and mother were tending their scattered flock.

Tomas's grandmother continued, panting, struggling for breath and for words. "There's going to be a memorial service… four days from now, this coming Sunday, the Lord's Day… at our church down the street. There will be no burial… there are no bodies… they won't have even a decent Christian burial. ….. I won't be able to attend the church service: I don't have it in me to be able to get to the church, but our priest will no doubt come to our house to pray with us.

"I have also asked around for a place for you to stay…Tomas, a place which will look after your needs, a place where you can grow… into adulthood, where you can learn a trade…. There is such a place, in our nearby city.

"*Babusya*, I don't want to leave you, I don't want you to send me away."

She pushed a stray lock of her hair away from her eyes, her hand gradually drifting back down to her lap.

"Listen, Tomas, my dear *onuk*, I have no choice, I have no other choice…. While you were sleeping, I went to our next-door neighbors, the Kravchenko's, and they told me about this place for you. In fact, after hearing what had happened to your parents, Pan Kravchenko was kindness itself.…. He rode over to that place on my behalf, and informed them of our existence, and came back with information for me.

"I think you realize that I'm in poor health, and I don't have long on this earth. As it is, I'm living solely on your dear grandfather's little pension, which he earned for working all those years in the weaving factory as a supervisor. That's the only thing keeping me from the poorhouse." She bit her lower lip. "Our family's very small. We have some relatives out east, at least… we had them before the war.…. I haven't heard anything from them since. The letters I sent to them were unanswered.…. They must have moved." She shrugged. "Who knows?"

Tomas placed one hand slowly into his other, cupping and encircling it protectively. He was by now realizing and accepting that his part-time parents would not be coming back, that he had no home to go back to. The home which he had occupied with his parents was next door to his grandmother's little home; their landlord had permitted his grandfather to construct it many years before Tomas was born.

"Pan Kravchenko told the man in charge at this place, a Pan Osterach, to arrange for a place for you.…." She looked balefully at Tomas, who continued to stare at her uncomprehendingly, she thought. "Do you... have you... heard what an orphanage is?"

Tomas's tongue was thick, his lips rigid; he found it difficult to get the words off of his tongue and out of his mouth. "*I think... I've heard... know 'bout... some children... no p-parents.*"

"That's right...." Tomas's grandmother was tired and anxious to get beyond the hurtful explanation. "It's a place where they will care for you. You will be with other children, boys and girls... who are also... who have no parents."

Tomas nodded, his eyes downcast. He was still hoping that his stoic grandmother would have a last-minute change of heart. But that, he soon realized, with the facts as she had presented them, was a vain hope.

His grandmother continued, wanting to put the topic to rest. She knew that Tomas would most definitively have preferred to remain with her under her roof, but she was adamant that he should move out. *It's for the best,* she had reasoned. She knew she was doing the right thing.

Once I'm dead, the orphanage would come for him anyway. Better now than later.

"From what I understand, the Principal will send someone to come and collect you, when we ask him to."

Tomas absorbed his grandmother's explanation. He didn't like what he had heard about orphanages; that they were like prisons where children were kept in terrible conditions and against their will. For a fleeting moment he thought about bolting from the house, running away.

But what good would that do for him? Where would he go? Where would he sleep? What about food? He didn't know much about the wide world out there, but he realized that there was nothing he could do to avoid the orphanage.

"Over the next several days, I'm going to pack your things in one of the cloth bags your father left behind. You can take one of your father's prayer books, if you like."

Tomas thought about that: yes, he would like one of his father's prayer books to remember him by. He nodded. "Can I also take a couple of my favorite books with me?"

"Yes, if they'll fit inside. Don't go loading up too much in the bag, mind you."

Later, before placing the worn books in his bag, he caressed them fondly, and shed a tear. He remembered the countless times his mother had read to him from those same books when he was little. He had received the books from his parents as birthday presents several years before. He knew the stories verbatim, but he never tired of having his mother read the stories to him.

A short while later, his grandmother gave him some thick, steaming porridge for breakfast, with some hot tea. They both ate by the stove.

Tomas was sent out to a little covered hut next to the outhouse where his father had stored firewood for the winter. He touched the wood, and felt a pang of nostalgia for his father. He gathered up a two-armful pile, which he deposited in a corner of the tiny kitchen.

He sat by the stove, watching the flames lick against the wrought-iron grille, trying not to think about the terrifying death his parents had encountered. He remembered once hugging his grandmother in a burst of exuberance while she just stood stoically by, her arms by her side.

His grandmother sat nearby in her chair. She drifted in and out of consciousness, mumbling in her sleep. After a while she arose with difficulty, her knuckles and her face white with the exertion. She hobbled over to the stove, where an old pot sat bubbling slowly. She removed a hooked ladle from the stove-side, and emptied a couple of ladlefuls of a pork-and-vegetable stew into two chipped soup plates and added a hunk of black bread for him to sop up the sauce that remained on his plate. He washed that down with a mug of hot tea his grandmother had placed in front of him.

Tomas tried to visualize what exactly was in store for him, but couldn't. The little world of comparative comfort and safety that he had counted upon had disappeared, never to return.

The next several days passed quickly. A stream of neighbors visited, paying their respects and offering condolences. Most came with offerings of food, which his grandmother accepted gratefully. The church service came and went; the priest came and prayed for the souls of the departed.

After the priest had left, Tomas's grandmother told him to be on his best behavior, because his parents' souls were in the house, and would be until the fortieth day.

"*How do you know that?*" Tomas had asked.

His grandmother leaned close. "Because until the fortieth day after their death they're restless, and they revisit where they had once been. Our priests tell us that." She looked around, her old eyes which had seen so much suffering wide with belief. "I feel their presence all around us."

Several more days went by. One day, his grandmother told him that she had packed everything inside his bag, in readiness for the emissary from the orphanage.

Tomas was alarmed; he was hoping that his move would still somehow be overlooked and that he would be spared. "*When will he come?*"

"Pan Kravchenko arranged it for tomorrow."

It was early afternoon of the following day, under a leaden, threatening sky, that they heard a horse and cart draw up outside.

A rap on the heavy door announced the arrival of the orphan-age's emissary.

Tomas answered the door, his grandmother just behind him.

"I'm from the institution, Pani, here to pick up a young person -" he consulted a piece of paper in his hand, and read out the name.

"Tomas, go and get your bag, and put on your winter coat."

Tomas was leaving the tiny shack when his grandmother pulled him back, giving him a hug and a kiss on his cheek. He noticed that she had tear-filled eyes; she whimpered softly as she said, *"Take good care of yourself, my dear boy… I'll try to keep in touch, for as long as I'm able."*

Tomas didn't remember much about the ride in to the orphan-age; he was in a daze. The muffled 'clip-clop' of the horse's hooves and the rhythmic swaying of the cart were hypnotizing, as the horse pulled faithfully through the snow and slush-filled streets, narrow and wide.

Upon arrival at the dark three-story house that was the orphan-age, the front door opened as he climbed the entry stairway. He noticed that on either side of the door there were open iron grilles with a large padlock attached. *A separate gate… to keep us inside… or to protect us.*

A youngish woman dressed in black silently beckoned him to follow her. She led him to a heavy paneled door, and knocked. Upon hearing a muffled response she opened it, and with a bent arm and pointing finger signaled that he enter.

At the far end of a large, dark-paneled room, a man sat behind a dark wooden desk. Behind the desk were two large bay windows, in the middle of which was a large stylized cross.

The strange man was tall and thin; he was dressed in black, apart from a stiff-collared white shirt which anchored his black tie. The man looked him up and down, scrutinizing him for any trace of emotion.

"Hello, young man. You must be Tomas… err… *Parenko,* correct? We've been expecting you. Put down your bag, and sit down over there."

Tomas did as he was told; he felt melancholy and lifeless, resigned to whatever happened to him. He looked down at his short stubby fingers, denying the man the opportunity to look into his eyes; he made a resolution to always look down in future. It was easier that way.

The man spoke with a gravelly voice, all the harsher due to the emptiness of his office. "Welcome to our institution, young man. This is your new home. We will educate you, feed you and help you, if you do what we say…. Do you see that door? Look at it—it symbolizes what we are here, and what we do.

"The top four panels over there represent the holy cross of Jesus, our faultless Messiah, under whom we go about our daily lives…. The bottom two panels represent an open

Bible, which we routinely use to find His truth, and abide by His instruction.

"You are to obey all instructions from our staff, whomever they may be. Discipline will be strictly enforced. My name is Pan Osterach: you will address me as Pan.

"Now, I want you to give me your full name, including your Saint's name, then your date of birth, and finally your former address."

Pan Osterach's quill hovered in mid-air; as Tomas began talking softly, his quill scratched as he wrote on a large ledger. *"And your former address?"*

Tomas reflected on the finality and closure of his former life. *I'm really in a scary place right now. I will forget about everything that happened before, forget about my parents, forget about my grandmother. I am alone in the world.*

Pan Osterach put his quill down and blotted the page; he then rang a bell which lay cupped on his desk. The office door opened, and in walked a heavy-set older woman dressed in black.

"This is our Head Matron, *Pani* Fedora. To you she will be *Pani*, always *Pani*. You are to show her your utmost respect. She will shortly take you to your room."

Pan Osterach walked over to a wooden lectern, on which rested a ledger; he opened it, his pointer finger went down a page, and then another. With a grunt, he made an entry in the book, and then closed it. He went over to a nearby cupboard and opened it, muttering to himself. The cupboard contained rows of keys, each with a brass fob and a colored tag. His hand hovered over a row of keys, and selected one.

"Three zero nine, Matron Fedora; two boys already in the room." He handed the key to the woman.

Pani Fedora led Tomas up two flights of stairs, waddling and breathing heavily as she climbed. The sounds of many voices, some in unison (*pupils in classes?*) and individual utterances wafted out to them, some male and some female. She held on to the shiny well-worn banisters, pulling herself up as she climbed. Tomas had difficulty negotiating the turns in the stairwell carrying his bag; a couple of times he had to stop and change hands.

Pani Fedora led him down a dimly-lit wood-floored corridor; the floor creaked as they walked. Solid doors stretched all the way down the corridor, to the right and to the left. She stopped at a door and opened it with a sharp click of the key in the lock.

The room contained two iron double bunk beds against the two side walls. Between the beds, a large iron cross hung, prominent against the white wall. There were a couple of tall closets in the corners.

"Put your bag in that closet for now. One of my Matrons will come to you later to go through your clothing. We label them all. On Mondays we wash dirty clothes."

She looked at the bunk beds, pointing to one. "Up there is a folded mattress—that's yours. One of my Matrons will bring you a pillow, a sheet a blanket and a towel." She looked at Tomas, noting how forlorn he appeared. "It's not that bad. Your roommates will explain our daily routine to you, and you'll settle in. What's your name?"

"Tomas."

"When did you lose your parents, Tomas?"

Tomas was taken aback. "I think… a while ago… last week."

"Oh, as recently as that…. Many of our boys and girls come to us from foster homes, where they didn't adjust…. Well, it happens to all of us, sooner or later."

Just then, a couple of boys spilled into the room; they stopped talking excitedly as soon as they saw *Pani* Fedora. She waved them in. "*I want you to meet your new roommate, Tomas.*"

The taller of the two nodded. "*My name's Petr.*"

The other, chubbier with tousled hair, raised a hand in greeting. "*I'm Olek.*"

Tomas nodded.

Pani Fedora looked at the three boys, her eyes steely, her mouth in a mirthless smile. "I'll leave you to it. Tell Tomas about the schedule, boys, so that he'll feel more at home."

She departed, closing the door.

Petr jumped onto his bed, scrutinizing Tomas. "*So tell me, what are you in for?*"

"What?"

Petr changed his question slightly, grinning. "*Why are you here?*"

Tomas began formulating a response, thinking carefully as he began to mouth his reply.

Olek chuckled. "*Of course* we know why you're here. But don't worry - you'll get used to it."

8

Our Paris Story

*I*t all began in the most surprising, unexpected way possible. My wife Sonia and I were at the airport, saying farewell to someone—my younger daughter, who had briefly visited the city of her birth while on a book tour, promoting her most recent book. The visit was short, and I regretted that I rarely got to see her anymore, ever since she had eschewed Miami and had moved to New York City and eventually to Washington DC, climbing onward and upward, on her way to becoming a note-worthy journalist.

My wife and I had grown accustomed to accompanying depart-ing friends and relatives to the airport out of consideration and our feeble attempt at prolonging our time with them until the next occasion they flew into town.

We had said our goodbyes, and were on our way toward an appropriate exit from the interminably long main concourse in the general direction of our parked car. The concourse seemed to be different in appearance than what I was accustomed to. *Was it the lighting?* Yes, the lighting was definitely off: the high-ceilinged lights were more muted than before. Also, the concourse itself had become narrower: what was happening? Was it my aging eyesight?

The distance between the airline desks and the stores and boutiques was narrower, causing the lines of travelers and visitors to spill into one another. There was a constant overflowing of travelers with luggage and others, moving endlessly in both directions. Even the porters were in on the unearthly illusory nebulousness; they gyrated in tune to the lively music behind their luggage trolleys, paying little heed to the passing of time. The lights flickered momentarily, then came back on in a reddish tint, then a garish blue.

Suddenly some disco music blared from the innumerable public address speakers, and incredibly, the concourse took on the appearance of a giant elongated nightclub, with some lights flickering on and off, while others threw powerful beams in all directions. The whole ambiance was surreal and bizarre.

Some people even set down their luggage and started dancing in the tight places between the seats and the two snaking rows of close-packed humanity.

"This is *incredible*," I said to Sonia. "Have you ever seen anything like this?" She negged slowly, shaking her head in disbelief.

"What's happened? This is absolutely *unreal*." For the first time I noticed several translucent, glazed and frameless advertising signs floating effortlessly high above our heads, almost as if they were wafting their pellucid gauzelike smoky messages across invisible air currents. Which they must have been. *"Visit romantic Paris, for the memories of a lifetime,"* read the nearest one hovering above our heads as it drifted slowly sideways.

"I've always wanted to go to Paris, but due to one thing or another, never did." said Sonia. "You've been many times, right?"

"Yes, but it's been quite a while since I last visited. I guess the only reason you and I never made it to Paris was that we had so many other places to see, all around the world," I mused. "Would be fun to go once again."

We had been a couple for more than twenty-two years, combining our lives when we were in our late fifties. Because Sonia came from Chile and had close relatives there, we had visited that South American country almost annually. We'd also been to South Africa a couple of times, to visit my sister and family. Interspersed with those visits, we'd also been on many other trips throughout the U.S. and Canada, as well as large swaths of Europe. Paris stood out, appealing to us even more because we'd never been as a couple.

"There's something about Paris that grabs me and doesn't let go," said Sonia, as she dodged around a stream of people moving past us. "It's like a *magnet* that's pulling me in. It's almost as if I lived a former life there."

"*Just Paris?*" I asked. "We've been almost everywhere else that we consider meaningful, you and I."

"Yes, only Paris." Sonia gazed at the wispy, beckoning and enticing Paris sign above our heads; a flashing silky and delicate gold-colored Eiffel Tower symbol now magically appeared inside the shimmering frame. "I've had this *overwhelming* desire to breathe the Parisian air since I was a little girl."

The concourse continued to manifest a strange and unusual appearance. This was surely not what we normally encountered when visiting the airport main concourse. There was definitely something eerie and ghostlike about it.

We had some difficulty in maneuvering amongst the masses of people who seemed to be either streaming in our direction or pressing us from behind, or else finding the time and the inclination to dance to the enveloping music blaring from invisible speakers.

Isn't it funny that we usually pay no attention to the endless blurry, indecipherable public announcements which airports worldwide are notorious for? And yet, the fuzzy, snarled lyrics and the tangled disorderly beat seemed to enhance the attraction of the music. *This is otherworldly, oneiric,* I thought. *Totally phantasmagoric! The familiar is now hovering in parts unknown possibly close by, but we are visiting another reality, somewhere we have never visited before.*

It's as if we'd been projected into another realm, an imaginary place, a never-never land. We were at the interstice of reality and unreality, between the contours of what is possible and what cannot actually occur; this wasn't the usual domain of consciousness we normally experience. This was paranormal.

Opposite a well-known airline's battery of desks, there was a sudden flurry of activity. This was happening 'between the lines' of the masses of people drifting to the right and the left.

Airline personnel were approaching passers-by in the streaming mass and asking them questions.

Suddenly, a ground-crew member pushed through the crowd and approached us as well. He was smiling and beaming with pleasure, his teeth showing through his moustache. I noticed that his tie was crooked and his airline cap was askew.

"'scuse me, sir, madam—*Paris*? Would you like to fly to *Paris*? We have a very limited number available seats, leaving for Paris in just three hours. Return trip exactly a week from today. Are you locals—where do you live? *Wonderful*—you could go home, pick up your passports and a roll-on each and be back in time. Very enticing, *Paris*—chance of a lifetime. You both can be on our flight to the City of Lights for just the cost of *one hundred fifty dollars each*! Round trip! Isn't that a bargain?"

My brain focused on the offer, and the necessity of making a decision. I looked at Sonia, who was as incredulous as I. Evidently, I was doing the same calculation that she was.

"Why's it so cheap?" I blurted defensively, expecting a catch, an excluding detail.

The airline employee chuckled. "We have a *heavy*—one of our big planes, coming off of maintenance, and flying back half empty. So we decided—the higher-ups did, actually—to fill the seats at a huge discount. She's flying back to Orly, and not CdG: Charles de Gaulle? *You win, we win.* At least we'll cover the cost of the flight. *Paris, yes or no?* If yes, pay us now so that we can hold the seats for you. *Chance of a lifetime!*"

Sonia and I exchanged glances. Her eyes said it all; they were sparkling with the anticipation. I cast another quick glance at Sonia. We had left in a real hurry with my daughter in order to make it to the airport on time. She was wearing a simple summery yellow dress with short sleeves. It was still pleasantly hot in our part of the world, whereas much of the northern hemisphere was slowly dropping into the months of bone-chilling cold, accompanied by the absolute need for four or five layers of clothing. On her feet she wore the quickest shoe item she could have found: a pair of unpretentious black pumps.

I had heard of family members of airline employees being charged just the taxes for a seat on an international flight. But this offer was almost as attractive. In my overworked brain, I did a quick analysis: One hundred fifty was possibly ten percent of the cost of a regular seat, round trip.

How incongruous. This is really a flight of fancy. What if we were to accept the offer… Paris!

Bizarrely, something from Barrie's Peter Pan flashed through my mind; '*The moment you doubt whether you can fly, you cease forever to be able to do it.*'

The City of Lights beckoned with a heretofore muted appeal, its compelling and magnetizing attractions suddenly displayed before us in lustrous detail. I muttered, more as an admonition than as a critique. "*How could we? We're not psychologically ready for an international destination right now, even if it is Paris.*"

Sonia added her two cents; she saw the possibilities. "What's really keeping us from doing this? *Passports*, plus the basics—toothbrushes, toothpaste, comb, hairbrush, changes of under-wear, sneakers, jeans, tee-shirts, blouses, shirts, jackets…. It's all doable in—what—*three hours*?"

"That's right, ma'am—you have three hours. Two seats—that'll be three hundred dollars." The disheveled ground crewman hooked his head toward the nearby airline desk. "Claudine over there'll take your payment. Congratulations!" *The moment you doubt whether you can fly….* Before I could restrain myself, I'd paid for the two seats. The closest emotion I could describe for my mood at that time was that I was in an irreverent daze. I felt a mixture of shock, wonder and frivolous anticipation, rather like a boy who thought he was being taken out for candy or ice cream, but finds that he's going to a fabulous circus instead. And possibly have the candy or ice cream in addition.

I didn't want to give up on the temptation of flying, even if the possibility of our boarding was so remote. Even the offer, as farfetched as it was to consider, was tempting in its having been made; I still couldn't believe that I was actually going through with it. *We were upstream, along the river of Time....* I remembered reading something from Heraclitus, something about a man never being able to step into the same river twice, because it's not the same river, and he's not the same man.

Claudine was courtesy itself. As my credit card was being approved and the receipt was then clattering through the processor, she smiled and said, "Now don't you be worried about going through baggage check and passport control: we have a priority line and agents to assist you. But make sure that you're here promptly." With that she handed me my receipt, looking me right in the eye, broadly smiling all the while.

Have you ever heard of being propelled toward something not quite meeting your rational approval, but nonetheless you do it? Maybe that's not really true, my being forced to do something unwillingly, I mean. But this was ridiculous! Ten minutes ago we were walking back towards our car, and now we're leaving for *Paris*—as in Paris, *France!*

The smiling ground crewman had been persistent, never accepting defeat. He knew that there would always be a percentage of passers-by at the airport who would jump at the opportunity

"What about hotels once we get there?" Sonia asked, not quite believing that she was asking a question quite like that. She's a level-headed, rational person, not at all influenced by peer pressure or other people's expectations. Under normal conditions, she's completely sensible; she has always lived within her means, never ever thinking about the futility of considering such a rushed and impractical flight of fancy. Nonetheless, she would have admitted to her having a healthy dose of incredulity and implausibility over what had just occurred. *"This is happening*—we're leaving for my never-never land," she exclaimed excitedly.

After being issued the two tickets for Paris, Sonia and I fought the oncoming rush of humanity until the nearest exit; the rest of the distance to our car was covered in double-quick time outside the suddenly mysterious and unfamiliar terminal.

The auto exit ramps were interminably slow; it was as if there was a plot by the drivers of other vehicles to obstruct us in our mission. By the time we got to the highway, almost an hour of our allotted three had passed. When we eventually got to our apartment, an hour-and-a-half had sped by.

I had the distinct feeling that time itself was being stretched and contracted simultaneously.

The challenge was to speedily put the necessary items into our individual roll-ons. Sonia was more adept at achieving this. But she did fling out helpful reminders: "Don't forget to take a couple of long-sleeved shirts and a sweater…. No, *not* a sweater… second thoughts: wear a *cardigan* under your jacket. You'll save space that way… easier to pull off…. Remember to pack your toothbrush and paste: we'll share your toothpaste."

Time sped by. I stuffed our passports in the inside pocket of my jacket. We found that time was dribbling away, with no ability to get ahead of it, to somehow control it…. Zipped up our roll-ons: unzipped both for forgotten items; eye-drops for Sonia, an extra pair of socks for me.

The trip back to the airport was a haze, a blurred slice of memory occupied by flashes of heavy traffic, garnering Sonia's admonishment for a too-quick cut-off, and finally finding a narrow parking place, made narrower by being between two SUV's.

We ran to the gate, our roll-ons' wheels bouncing around and almost sparking behind us. We were ushered into a secure line for a baggage inspection, and then taken over to passport control. It all happened in a whirl of activity and bustle beyond our control, all surrounded by other commotion taking place in a tense area where one is aware that travelers are in a heightened sense of awareness — and stress. Our adrenaline pushed us past the tension parameters; I developed a pounding headache.

Getting to the sleek, powerful jet awaiting us was a blur of early activity and then suddenly non-activity. Sonia, always ready with home remedies and sensible solutions, dispensed a couple of Tylenol with some water. We settled in to our seats, lulled into a wordless stupor by the torrent of events, rupturing conventional norms. My feelings felt like a primordial lake which due to a cloudburst of biblical proportions had burst its terrestrial boundaries, overflowing, and was now rushing forward, darting, dashing, surging, engulfing new territory, released from its confines, following the contours of the land into vast spaces which had not experienced wave upon wave of flooding water ever before.

I was now in uncharted waters, a place where disorder and harmony clashed, measuring the dissonance between rival elements. A thought flashed through my mind: *You won't be able to fly unless you believe, and take a giant leap.*

I closed my eyes and drifted off into a dreamless, impenetrable sleep. Without my knowing about it, we were airborne. Sonia nudged me awake, although I resisted coming back from where I was. She told me that they were serving dinner, and did I want something to eat and drink. I ate the dinner, which proved to be quite appetizing.

Sometime later, after the dinner refuse had been collected, I put on my blackout mask and fell into a fitful, erratic sleep, my hands buried in my lap and my head pressed up against the backrest. Then I suddenly dropped into a zone of profound unconsciousness. I felt as if I was in a long, dark tunnel, being propelled forward at lightning speed. I no longer felt a part of the plane; I didn't even feel the seat under me, or feel Sonia by my side. I thought that I was all alone in limitless space, shooting forward so fast that I didn't wobble or waffle; I didn't even notice my breath, or whether I was even breathing. I felt myself rocketing forward in a tight vacuum, somehow feeling the presence of whatever was out there pulling me forward, guiding my trajectory. Nothing was present; I didn't even know that I was existent, but the immutable Force was smoothly, unerringly speeding me forward with no deviation from wherever my being was headed toward.

I had no understanding of time, or time elapsing. Night and day were meaningless constructs. I was enveloped in darkness, and darkness reigned, alone and supreme. I must have woken up and fallen asleep several times, but the difference between the two was insignificant. All my ears discerned in the fleeting moments of wakefulness was a gentle persistent humming sound, which added to my feeling of isolation.

Suddenly I felt a slight downward pull, as if my extreme forward motion in some kind of unflinching straight line had taken a slightly lower direction. It was a supernatural experience, not like anything I'd ever undergone before. The first I knew that I was not alone in limitless void somewhere in the cosmos was when I was gently shaken. I resisted the intrusion, thinking to myself that I was being interfered with, that this would prevent me from reaching my assigned destination. I gradually pulled out of one reality and into another, although it took some indefinite time to grasp the transition. It was Sonia, softly whispering, telling me that coffee was being served, with tea plus other options. I was mindful of where I was, but my thoughts were erratic. *At thirty thousand feet*, I thought, *the mind has plenty of space to wander.*

"They're starting to serve breakfast up in First Class: I can see the carts moving down the aisle," Sonia's disembodied voice reached my brain. "Are you awake?"

I made an effort and roused myself from my stupor, pulling the mask off, and wincing in the bright light that the airline crew had turned on. I breathed in the air that my lungs evidently had been deprived of.

"I was worried about you, *Corazon*," Sonia said quietly. "Every time I glanced at you, it looked as if you had checked out of this world."

I smiled wanly. "You have no idea how close you are to the truth."

"What d'you mean?"

I sighed; it was a long sigh, a sigh of release, of roominess after the restrictive headlong flight through incredibly limitless open-spaced universe of oblivion, aloneness and isolation. "I've just experienced the most surreal journey of my life, at least that's how I can best describe it. A journey within a journey. While sitting here beside you in this plane."

"Maybe it was your headache, and the effect of the Tylenol I gave you," suggested Sonia.

I swallowed, not entirely convinced. "Never before." I shrugged hard, as if trying to clear the fog from my brain.

"Anyway, *Corazon*, we're about an hour and twenty minutes out of Orly Airport. The pilot just announced that over the intercom."

I absorbed the information, still not quite getting my head around what had occurred to me during the hours that I had been all alone in limitless space. I mulled over the uncanny experience I had. "D'you know, sweetie—I think that this completely unexpected trip is going to be one to remember for the ages. There's something *otherworldly* about it."

Sonia thought about what I had said, but added brightness to my somber mood. "Well, we're about to land in a beautiful, interesting place that I've had a connection with since I was a small girl in Punta Arenas. Back then, I even learned French in preparation for a trip which never happened—*until it happened*!"

The next hour was a whirl of activity. We were flying over land; here and there I could see the bunched lights of civilization below. Little villages, towns and cities flashed signals in the languorous predawn with their lights and then vanished behind us. More dark spaces, punctured by lights. Suddenly we encroached upon an intricate giant web of lights ahead of us, suddenly surrounding us. It was as if the myriad sparkling lights had become *everything*, occupying the whole world. *Paris*! This must be Paris!

The plane banked slowly over the city at the time that it was still enveloped in darkness, with tens of thousands of lights, web-like, sparkling in the predawn. The broad avenues and smaller streets were all illuminated like dendritic strings of shining effervescent pearls, glowing their promise of exotic excitement and rapture in this city of iridescent lights and fervent dreams.

The pilot explained that he was able to fly over Paris so that his passengers could see the panoramic splendor below because the flyover occurred a few minutes after the end of the nighttime restriction. Tongue-in-cheek, with a pronounced twinkle in his voice, he gave a disclaimer. "Please don't think that I *planned* to fly in a little slower so that we could take in Paris in all its predawn glory…. It just happened that way, folks."

We could see all the major landmarks: The Eiffel Tower; Notre Dame Cathedral; the *Arc de Triomphe*, with all of its wide arterial avenues lit in full splendor, all were laid out in astonishing detail to the delighted '*oohs*' and '*ahhs*' of passengers as we all ogled the magnificent display beneath us.

"We've arrived—*Paris!*" Sonia exclaimed, her eyes ablaze with excitement. "My eternal dream has actually come true. And to think—it took a chance offer at the airport to get us here."

Peter Pan's words flitted back to me. "*The moment you doubt whether you can fly….*"

"Whatever it took, we took it." I retorted.

The deplaning formalities were tedious, the same as any other place, no matter where in the world one arrives. It's an imposition to afflict this punishment—cruel but unfortunately very usual— on international travelers…. Baggage claim for some; Baggage check, passport control, the long march to ground transportation. The only difference to us was that the airport personnel spoke French. We were no longer in the United States; we were in an exotic, historic French-speaking country.

Orly looked and behaved basically the same as any other huge international airport, but with a distinctive Gallic twist.

By the time we dragged our roll-ons outside to look for ground transportation, our resolve to try a shuttle, or possibly a train with a change somewhere down the track, or a bus to somewhere in the city (and then what?) had dissipated and vanished.

"*A taxi…* I don't care what the cost is," Sonia said. "I'm *pooped.* I'm not as young as I used to be."

We hailed a cab, rather, a cab rolled up in front of us. The driver knew right away that we weren't French.

The only thing he had to discern was where we were from. We entered, our roll-ons with us.

He looked back at us with expectation and a hint of inquisitiveness. "*Où aller?*"

For a moment, I must admit that my high-school French completely deserted me. I looked quickly at Sonia, and I could see a calm resolve in her eyes. "*Vers la Ville, a Paris, s'il vous plait.*"

I smiled at her; I was impressed. "Good job, honey."

"Almost the same in Spanish, with a slight difference."

"*Vive la petite différence.*"

The driver quickly looked back at us in his rearview mirror as he merged with the traffic leaving the airport. "*Vous etes anglais?*"

"*Non, nous sommes Americains,*" I blurted, happy to be practicing my French once again.

Sonia also determined to add to her success. "*Nous n'avons pas un place pour rester. Pouvez-vous nous*—how do you say?"

The driver found inspiration. "*Ahh, oui—un* endroit, *un place, pour rester?*"

"*Si*—I mean *oui!*" Sonia slipped into three languages in her delight that the driver understood.

I decided to weigh in. "*Un bon endroit, mais pas trop cher.*"

The driver smiled in his rearview mirror. "*Bien, je t'emmenerai dans un bel endroit.*"

On such petty things are international relations enhanced! I was proud of our linguistic abilities.

The highway the driver took us down was full of industrial warehouses and commercial buildings, and after that pretty countryside, cows and little villages. Eventually, the outskirts of Paris flashed into view. In the distance, I saw a thrilling sight: It was the Eiffel Tower, front and center!

"Look, sweetie, look!" I pointed with a straight index finger.

"Oh, wow! *We must be in Paris!*" was all that Sonia could say, her eyes absorbing the view.

We approached the city, with its orderly yet disorderly layout, with buildings the same height that probably were a couple of hundred years old—maybe more—many with statues and intricate latticework adorning them. The streets were complex, many of them very narrow, yet well-thought-out. The city planners had instilled the city with enduring beauty while permitting traffic to somehow find its necessary way through, using one-way streets in areas created when horse-drawn traffic was customary. We crossed the Seine across an impressively decorated bridge, and entered the Marais District. From my previous visits to Paris, I recalled that the neighborhood had been a haven for the Jewish community, going back to Napoleon's time, when Jews became emancipated into the larger population.

"This is—or was—the old Jewish neighborhood of Paris," I told Sonia. "But there are many restaurants, cafes, bakeries, butcher shops and stores which still maintain a Jewish presence."

Our cab driver peered at us through his rearview mirror: he had been listening avidly. "*Mais oui—c'est un joli domaine. Je t'emmenerai a l'hotel.*"

We visited three hotels of various sizes, and finally a couple of bed-and-breakfasts, with no success; we had the driver wait for us each time. There was no room at the inn.

The driver put a finger to his temple as if to indicate something important. "*J'ai un idea. Ça peut marcher.*"

"He thinks he has an idea that could work," Sonia muttered.

Our driver drove past *Rue des Rosiers*; I scrunched down to see where we were going. "That street was one of the Jewish community's main streets. Like a lot of other European cities, impoverished arriving Jews from other parts of Europe flocked to low-rent areas which were close to railroad stations from countries further to the east. This area's beautiful and historic, but it was cheaper to live here than in other sections of town."

The driver swung the cab around a corner and into a cul-de-sac. Up ahead was a three-story house painted light blue, with a gabled roof.

"*C'est un B&B, moins connu. Voyons voir.*" The driver decided to practice his English. "Thees ees a B&B, not so *populaire*, not so *notoire*. We see."

We got out, dragging our roll-ons behind us. The first object I noticed was a little circular enamel blue-and-white plaque, with the words 'Bed and Breakfast' emblazoned on it.

"That's reassuring," I said to Sonia. "Now all we have to find out is whether they have a room for us."

We knocked on the front door; there were two little rectangles of lawn on either side, bordered by neatly arranged flower beds and little hedges, now all victims of the slow descent into winter. We waited anxiously. Finally an elderly lady appeared; we could see her approaching through the little opaque window in the door.

"*Oui? Je peux vous aider?*"

Small and stout, with her short white hair arranged around a pleasant face, she stood quizzically looking at us in her paisley-styled housecoat, smiling a friendly smile.

Noticing our hesitation in finding the appropriate words, she changed her approach. "You are *touristes*, yes? Where are you from?"

"From the United States, from Miami."

"Ah, Miami in America... *quel charme*. You are looking for a room?"

I thought that a question like hers was positive, that there may actually be a room for us. "Yes, yes of course. Do you have one, a room for us, that is?"

She rubbed her hands on a dish-towel she was carrying. "I don't see why *not*," she said to our happy relief. "The B&B is officially closed presently, but for you, *pourquoi non*?" She smiled and stepped aside. "Come in, come in, and make yourselves at home."

I quickly paid the driver, giving him an extra-large gratuity for solving our lodging problem.

The elderly lady took us to a back bedroom on the ground floor. The floor creaked pleasantly, welcoming us with every step we took. It was large and nicely furnished, with a bathroom off to one side.

"So what do you think, it's nice, eh?"

We walked around, getting the feel of the room. It was well-lit, with windows on two sides. Borne out of habit, I sat on the bed, and found it just right. "*Goldilocks*," I intoned. The elderly lady smiled approvingly.

Sonia walked over to the bathroom, pushed the door open, and peered inside. She admired the blue -bordered tiles, noting the slight smell of bleach. "I like it—it even has a bidet."

I looked in on the bathroom. More accustomed to French plumbing, I noted that we in the States are still far ahead of the Europeans, especially the French, in plumbing design and efficiency.

The elderly lady looked on approvingly. "So shall I say that you are my guests?"

There and then we settled on the price and the duration of our stay. We gave her our names.

"Please call me Noemie—that's the name I have used for a number of years; that in itself is a long story. You do not have to register... I know who you are, and I knew that you would come."

I was about to ask what she meant by that, but didn't. *Is she mistaking us for some other couple?*

She fished in her apron pocket and pulled out a key. "This is your key... I will leave you alone, you must be tired. Breakfast will be served when you give me indications that you are ready."

"Are there any other guests in the house?" Sonia asked.

"*Non*, none... Monsieur Beck gave refunds and found other accommodations for all the expected guests. He was *desperate*... he had to do it due to his and Madame Beck's sudden departure."

I was intrigued. "Why did they have to leave?"

"Ahh, *Alors*...Madame Beck's mother suddenly became ill in Normandy. She got a call from her brother begging her to come right away, so Monsieur Beck decided to accompany her there. They've always done things together." She pursed her lips in a resolute manner. "So they left me in charge in their absence."

Sonia looked at me. "I think we'd better relax. I'm starting to feel our overnight trip."

"Ah, then I'll leave you. Is there anything I can get for you, a cup of soothing tea, perhaps?"

"No, thank you."

"Ah, *bon*. If you want to go out later, for an afternoon snack or dinner, *peut etre*, there are many fine restaurants, some just around the corner. The one I would recommend for you, is called *Le Coq Qui Rit*, it's just around the corner."

"'The Rooster Who Laughs,'" I said, smiling. "That sounds like '*Cocorico*,' the sound the French say the rooster makes."

"Yes, that is so." Noemie smiled. "My second husband Marcel and I used to own it, a long time ago, before I retired. It's still very well run, by good friends."

"Great… we'll keep it in mind."

Sonia and I dozed, then were awake, and then dozed some more. Towards evening—it was already dark—we finally, bravely, decided to venture out. At half-speed, we struggled against jet-lag, and found a quite café, where we ate a muffin and a fruit salad with our tea.

On our way back, retracing our steps, we found that the cul de sac had a name; close to a small street lamp, we saw a nameplate: "*Place des Enfants Perdus.*"

"Hmm," I reflected. 'Place of Lost Children': I wonder what's the significance of that.

The next morning was rainy; a heavy rainfall was predicted by the news on television. We heard noises coming from the kitchen. We were almost ready to come out of our room when we heard a gentle knock on the door. It was Noemie, telling us that breakfast was served, and explaining where the first-floor dining room was.

When we sat down to eat, we found a small circular table to our liking, instead of the two larger tables in the room. Noemie bustled in, still wearing her apron over a paisley dress.

She offered us tea or coffee; we both chose coffee. It appeared more appropriate, here in Paris. As she poured our coffee (*au lait*), she asked us what we would like to eat. "Would you like a typical American-style breakfast, or would you want to be...*aventureux*, and try something typically French?"

I looked at Sonia. "Well, we're here in Paris, right sweetie? How about something from here... not too spicy, though."

Noemie beamed. "*Bon* — I'll start you with some *baguettes* and *tartines*, with butter and *confiture*.... Regarding your eggs, what I suggest is a typical French breakfast 'sandwich,' which is really a breakfast delicacy. Do you object to ham or cheese with your eggs? *Non*? As I said, it's a sandwich: it's called '*Croque Madame*,' meaning 'bite, or crunch, the lady'."

"Not too spicy?"

"*Non*, not spicy at all. But *delectable*." She smacked her lips with her spliced finger-endings.

"Okay, let's try it."

Noemie smiled and went into her kitchen, bringing out a tray full of mouthwatering French breakfast items, made certain that everything was to our liking, and then returned to her kitchen. We could smell the aroma of her cooking; it smelled *divine*.

She returned after ten minutes or so, with what I took to be a glorified cheese sandwich. Boy, was I wrong! *'Croque Madame'* was delicious, crunchy in the mouth, flavorsome grilled cheese in an exquisite sauce, thin-sliced ham and a not-quite-firm cheese. All the above was bookended by crunchy buttered toast, topped with a grilled sunny-side-up egg. To say that it was mouth-watering and appealing would be a huge understatement.

Sonia munched hers, her expressive eyes reflecting her enjoyment.

In my culinary rapture I forgot my table manners and asked Noemie for the recipe, with my mouth still partially full.

"I'm so happy that you like it. *'Croque Madame'* has a slightly runny fried egg-yolk on top, but *'Croque Monsieur'* is prepared without the egg. I gave you both the 'lady' variety. You can look it up, and make your own, if you are so inclined."

Once we had finished breakfast, Sonia asked Noemie what activity she would recommend on a rainy day.

She suggested visiting some museums. "The Louvre is *magnifique*, and the Centre Georges Pompidou for Modern Art, they are close by, as well as the *'Shoa* Memorial Museum' if you are in the mood. I myself have never seen it; it brings back terrible memories."

Sonia nodded. Intrigued, she asked a question that had been playing in her mind. "What is the significance of the name of this little cul-de-sac?"

"Ahh," said Noemie. "That deserves a full explanation. It may take some time; do you have it?"

We both mouthed our agreement.

"*Bon*…. This is something that grabs onto my heart, and refuses to release me." She sighed, as if steeling herself for an exertion. "During the war years, the Second War, France of course was conquered by the *Boches*, the Nazis. All of this is something everybody knows.

"But what happened *here*, in the northern part, was that the Nazis ruled with terrible cruelty and an iron fist, and with French anti-Semitic collaborators helping them, they started rounding up those Jews who tenaciously remained in Paris, instead of fleeing south. Conditions weren't much better down in the south, which was administered by collaborators, but at least the Nazis weren't as visible and active, unlike up here.

"The Jews they rounded up here were sent to *Drancy*, to the north-east of where we are, not too far away. This was a *horrendous* internment camp, and the Nazis shipped the innocent, unfortunate Jews out of there—in packed cattle-cars—to their death camps to the east, mostly in Poland." She looked at us to see whether we were following her. Reassured, she continued.

"What happened there, in Drancy, as well as many other places throughout Europe was an *indictment—un acte d'accusation—* a horrible crime, against all of humanity. Over sixty-seven thousand French Jews, including more than *six thousand* children were shipped out of Drancy in brutal conditions, to the death camps."

Noemie swallowed her tears and composed herself. "One of those children was mine. Little Danielle was four years old when her father, my dear husband Isaac, took her shopping in a little town near the German border where we lived at the time. This was in August of 1944."

I thought to myself... let's see... she was a young mother then, possibly... say, twenty in 1944... add fifty-six years to reach the year 2000. So she'd be seventy-six plus the years since 2000. No way—she can't be more than ninety years old! She looks like a spry seventy, or seventy-five at most.

We were spellbound by Noemie's story; she continued.

"Danielle was not a part of the Drancy statistic. She and Isaac were picked up at the time the Nazis were in full retreat, running like the brutal cowards they were, back to where they came from. But the *Einsatzgruppen*—the Death Squads—were still active even though the Nazis were in full flight. Can you possibly imagine: *the army was no longer functional*, but the *death squads were still intent on eliminating Europe's Jews....*

"Isaac had forged papers, but somehow they discovered the forgery and that he was Jewish, and little Dani was with him, so they grabbed them both."

Noemie stifled her tears, sobbing, heaving. Sonia spoke up, her voice full of compassion. "Noemie, if this is too difficult for you, maybe—"

Noemie smiled through her tear-filled eyes. "*Non*—this is *cathartique*. I have survived too much in the shadows of an alternative world. It's *helpful* to talk about these tragedies.... So that is the reason I fought so hard for the local *commune* to grant me my wish and have a memorial plaque, not just to honor little Dani, but for all those children who died so inhumanely, so tragically."

Noemie brushed some imaginary crumbs from her apron, and smiled away her unhappy memories.

"*Alors*, you have a whole day of museums in front of you. You could walk there. Tomorrow the weather will be pleasant and clear—then you can go to the Eiffel Tower, and after that to the *Arc de Triomphe*, and the Notre Dame Cathedral also awaits you as well. The easiest way to go, I believe, would be by Metro. *Boring*, I know, but it'll get you where you want to go quickly and efficiently."

Sonia and I borrowed an umbrella from Noemie, and set out for the Louvre. I remembered the route quite well; the waiting lines moved at a good pace, and we spent the remainder of the day in the museum. There was so much to see, according to our Louvre guide booklet, but we managed to see most of what we had wanted to see.

The sheer opulence of the former royal palace was impressive. We spent probably three hours in the various galleries before lunch, and went back for more afterwards. Apart from the beautiful landscape and portrait paintings, as well as the one-of-a-kind *objets d'art*, the ceiling paintings and intricate decorations were stunning in their magnificence.

For lunch, I had wanted to experience the famous Café Richelieu, which I had missed the last time I was in Paris, while still married to my first wife, so we indulged ourselves. We found a table on the covered, high-ceilinged terrace facing the famous giant glass pyramid, and we thoroughly enjoyed a typical Parisian meal plus a flavorsome glass of Bordeaux wine each, while protected from the rain.

It had stopped raining by the time we left the Louvre, so we walked home down Rue de Rivoli and up Boulevard Sebastopol, passing the huge modernistic Pompidou Center along the way.

Parisian streets are such a treat to walk through; every single street has a charm and attraction of its very own and a history that it was anxious to share with the casual observer. It was dark by the time we got home.

We had stopped in the Marais for a snack and a soft drink. Noemie bustled over and insisted on giving us some of her freshly baked '*macarons*,' with a cup of *café au lait*.

"Our *macarons* are a national specialty, *better* than the Italian version, because we put in more tasty almond paste, and less sugar...tell me how you like them." "Delicious!" we both exclaimed simultaneously.

We told Noemie about our day; it was good to summarize our feelings with a knowledgeable and empathetic third party.

Noemie grew expansive. "There's so much to see. The sheer number of museums *somme enorme*." She swung her arms in half-circles for emphasis. "But museums and still more museums would make your visit to this *ville magnifique* simply boring! Tomorrow, go first to the *Tour Eiffel*. It is worth the money."

Sonia nodded, thinking about something else.

"Noemie, you mentioned that you've used your first name only for a short time... why is that?"

"Ahh... that opens up a whole Pandora's box regarding the French attitude about foreigners—*personnes étrangères*. This may be the home of *liberté, d'Égalité et de Fraternité*. But the whole thing is basically a lie. That may astonish you, but '*l'habit ne fait pas le moine*,' which is to say, 'don't judge a book by its cover.'"

I noticed that Noemie had grown very intense; she sat with her hands intertwined on the table.

"True, *mes bons amis*, France has a tradition of equality, begun by the Emperor Napoleon in all of his conquered lands throughout Europe. He advocated *egalité* for all of his subjects. He actually had the *temerity* to emancipate the Jews. But still, you cannot undo centuries of racial discrimination and religious intolerance by means of an edict.

"I will give you one of many examples of blatant anti-Semitism perpetrated by the Church. Remember that for centuries priests and bishops spoke out from the pulpit of their churches about how the Jews had committed deicide by killing Jesus, and that they were perfidious and untrustworthy.

"Money collecting in the form of taxes and money lending were the only trades allowed to the Jews of those times, because the Church forbade Christians from charging interest. "Nowadays we know that the Jews back then — more than two thousand years ago — *didn't* kill Jesus. The Romans saw him as an agitator and a trouble-maker, and together with tens of thousands of other Jewish young men, he was crucified, the Roman form of capital punishment.

"Even worse, over the centuries the Church caused the deaths of countless numbers of Jews all over Europe by *scapegoating* — is that how you say it? — Jews and Judaism.

"*Alors*, when you go to Notre Dame Cathedral, pay particular attention to the two large statues above the main portico. On the left-hand side, you will see a depiction of a saintly '*Eclesia*,' representing the beauty of Christianity. On the right-hand side, you will see a depiction of a poor ragged woman representing Judaism. She's called '*Synagoga*,' and she's blinded by a snake wrapped around her eyes and her head, and her staff is broken. That's how the Church indoctrinated and influenced the masses against Jews.

"And these same depictions exist in many churches throughout France and elsewhere."

I interjected. I was a history major, with a very good understanding of European history. "France wasn't the only country in Europe with a long history of anti-Semitism. Germany and Austria come to mind -"

Neomie smiled a quiet smile, full of understanding; behind the smile was the steel backbone of history. "*Mais oui*, I grant you that. But only in France does this situation continue openly to the present time. It is *virulent*, and becoming worse. We not only have *home-grown* anti-Semites, but we also have *imported* Jew-haters, due to the influx of disenfranchised *Maghrebin,* North African Moslems, primarily those who are young, unemployed and looking for trouble.

"But behind the official laws, anti-Semitism ranked supreme, especially when it came to religion and the French Army.

"You remember the Alfred Dreyfus story, correct? Well, the French nation was *cut in half*, even after he was found to be innocent. *Half* the French nation didn't want to impugn the French Army — *mettre en doute* — and opted to cover up his innocence and insist on his continuing unjust imprisonment.

"It took a massive campaign by Emile Zola to press for Dreyfus' release. But the nation was evenly divided, with the Church siding with the army. This vehement reluctance to exonerate Dreyfus was a festering cancer that infects France even today.

"Then there's also the Churches' influence on the naming of children. Until a hundred years ago, all first names had to be biblical names, or names *officially approved* by the Church. And until the laws were relaxed in the 1970s, you were not permitted to name your baby any name you wanted.

"Now with the enormous immigration of Moslems from primarily North Africa, plus the more than half-million Jews, things are different.... But the Church and the Army are still very respected institutions which control modern France."

I nodded in agreement. "The Church swayed public perceptions throughout Europe. Sermons from the pulpit helped the rise of Fascism and Nazism by whipping up opposition to Jews and supposed Jewish influence. Many *pogroms* were initiated in churches."

She shifted in her chair, as if deciding how to say something. "*Oui*, that's all true…. As for me, I've swung around in full circle, as they say. When I was young, I wanted *nothing* to do with Judaism— it repelled me. Then I married a Jew—Isaac, my first husband, but he was 'bland'; not religious at all.

"He's the reason I speak English, because he was originally from London. After the tragedy of his and our daughter's death, eventually I moved to Paris, where I met and married Marcel, who was completely agnostic."

A few seconds of silence drifted by. It was as if Noemie was summoning the courage to say something that was inside her chest, dying to get out.

"My real name is *Sarah*—born Sarah Stein…. For many years in my small town I denied my Jewish background. I pretended that my family name was *German*, of all things! And then came the Nazi invasion….

"It was fortunate that my first husband Isaac arrived in town as a school teacher, or I would probably have married a *goy*—which I did later, anyway. But I didn't like the name 'Sarah.' I had to wait until the 'seventies to legally change my name to 'Noemie.' I've always liked the name, don't ask me why."

"What happened to you when… when your little girl and your husband were taken?" Sonia asked.

Noemie's expressive eyes darted from side-to-side, as if she were reliving the past. "I was *frantic*. My parents used some influence to discover *where* they had been taken. *Malheureusement*, they were taken and crammed onto a transport—*a cattle car*—bound for Poland. This was one of the last 'round-ups' of Jews before the *Boches* were driven across the border back to Germany. *I was destroyed*.... I couldn't leave the house for many weeks. I and my parents went into hiding; non-Jewish friends of ours helped us hide under a barn until the Americans and the British drove the Germans over the border."

"What happened to you after the war?"

"*Alors*, I tended to my parents, who were old and frail. After they died, I buried them in the little Jewish cemetery in our town, and left for Paris.... I met Marcel, and we became a couple; we were very compatible, with the same outlook on life and the same objectives.

"Eventually we got married, and together we worked in a restaurant until we had enough money to buy it from the owner. That's the *Coq Qui Rit*, still going strong here in the Jewish area, just around the corner. We catered to *everyone*, Jews and non-Jews alike. We weren't kosher. We used ham in our cooking, and served dairy products with meat. We were successful because of the quality of our food, and the friendliness of our service.

"Over the years I became an advocate for Jewish rights: human rights too, but especially *Jewish* rights, because I realized that even in this supposedly enlightened world, we have far too many enemies."

I nodded in agreement. "It amazes me sometimes about how frenzied and fanatical the anti-Semites are in blaming the Jews for everything."

Noemie concurred. "Thank goodness not everyone's like that. There are good people everywhere. We just have to find one another. Take my husband Marcel: he was a good man, honest and hardworking. I felt devastated when he died, many years ago. Eventually I decided to sell our restaurant to some dear friends, and retired."

"And then you came here, to the bed-and-breakfast."

"*Vraiment*—and then I came here."

Sonia and I were speechless. Like everybody else, we'd heard countless Holocaust stories, but here was a living, breathing survivor. Noemie reminded me of my great-aunt Rose, who was a medical doctor in her little town in a quiet corner of Germany before the Nazis came, then was sent to a concentration camp for 'good Jews'—those who had served the German Volk. After she was liberated, she continued to live in post-war West Germany for a time (to the great embarrassment of German bureaucrats), before emigrating to Israel, where she and I had many conversations about life and survival.

Noemie looked at our glum faces. "There's an idiom that come to mind at a time like this: '*Tout est bien qui finit bien.*'"

"All's well that ends well," I said, perking up.

"*Exactement!*" exclaimed Noemie. "We should always look on the bright side…. How about a little *apéritif*? I have a bottle of red Dubonnet just *waiting* for this occasion! Good, I'll go and get it."

As Noemie poured the wine, she looked at both of us, a smile on her face. "Here's another appropriate idiom: '*La vie est trop courte pour boire du mauvais vin.*'" She waited for us to translate.

Sonia began. "Life is… too short -"

And I finished: "– for drinking bad wine!"

"*Fantastique!*" exclaimed Noemie happily.

We clinked aperitif glasses, and Noemie said "'*Tchin—Tchin*'— that means 'Cheers.'"

"Tchin—Tchin", we repeated.

"So tomorrow, you go to the *Tour Eiffel*. I recommend that you get up early, around seven. How are you for climbing? *Bon*—no objection?... Then I suggest that you climb the steps to the first floor, to avoid the crowd: it involves a little over three hundred steps. Less crowded, and less expensive that way…. So I'll wake you up at seven, and I'll have a breakfast prepared for you, the usual, plus two '*Croques Madame.*'"

"That'll be wonderful. We're so happy to have met you," exclaimed Sonia. "You're making this Paris trip such a memorable one for us."

Noemie got up out of her chair and curtseyed slowly. "You are my very special guests. I am honored. For now, *bonne nuit*—I will see you tomorrow morning."

Sonia and I went to the Eiffel Tower, and after that, went to the Notre Dame Cathedral, and the *Arc de Triomphe*. We walked the whole length of the Champs—Elysees. We bundled up and took a cruise on the River Seine. We took a trip to see the Palace of Versailles—all the things that Paris is famous for.

Paris revealed her bewitching charm more than willingly, casting an ensorcelled spell over us. She—and we—behaved rather like children on Christmas morning, eyes diffused with the wonder of it all, confronted by so many colorfully wrapped boxes and packages, and opening one after the other in the sheer exhilaration of the joy of living.

But Sonia and I agreed that among our favorite moments were our evening conversations with Noemie; she was a force for all that is good and wholesome in life, a welcome relief from a complicated world.

On our last full day in Paris, Noemie told us to come back to the bed-and-breakfast for a special farewell dinner.

"I've *rarely* done this, but I'm going to cook dinner especially for you."

She outdid herself; when we came back from our final walk around the Marais, she served us a candle-lit dinner. First she served us shredded vegetables, with a gentle ginger flavor; then asparagus soup; then grilled salmon with crispy roasted potatoes and *haricots verts amandine* (green beans with shaved almonds); then an assortment of French cheeses washed down with Cabernet Sauvignon; sweet *crêpes* with a strawberry sauce, and finally *café au lait*.

We were sated with all these epicurean delights. What a simply glorious meal!

Filled with good food and bolstered by the knowledge that Noemie was a friend, Sonia asked her whether she had followed up to find what had happened to Isaac and little Danielle after they were snatched by the Nazis.

Noemie grew pensive, as if she were going back to those terrible times. Her eyes flickered, moving as if in a trance. "*Oui. J'ai cherche avec diligence dans les dossiers qui sont été rendus disponibles....* I turned the records upside down. I was obsessed. I wanted those damned Nazis to spit out the truth, that they had brutally murdered my family, my dear ones. Dani with her precious face and her curly hair was so sweet and innocent. She and Isaac didn't ... didn't deserve their horrible fate, not at all ... not at all.

"I found the records. Those cursed *Boches* kept meticulous records, the Devil take them.... They are recorded as having been gassed on the third of September, nineteen forty-four."

"*My birthday*, the day I was born!" Sonia gasped.

Noemie's eyes focused on Sonia, blanketing her in a warmth of raw emotion.

"That's why you came to me. I was waiting for you."

"*Wha*—what d'you mean?" Sonia exclaimed, astonished.

Noemie continued smiling, her eyes emoting pure love. "I believe in the transmigration of souls... the cycle of rebirth is eternal. You don't have to believe, it's enough that I do. My journey is complete."

The three of us continued talking, about this, about that. There were tears welling in Sonia's eyes.

Eventually, Noemie announced that she was tired, and wanted to wash the dinner dishes and go to bed. We offered to help. But she wouldn't budge.

"*Mes amours precieux*, I will not hear of it: it is for me to do. I will get up early to pack a breakfast for you to eat before your flight back to Miami. You won't see me tomorrow, because I am being called away. Tomorrow evening, Monsieur et Madame Beck will be back from Normandy, and the bed-and-breakfast will resume regular bookings."

Sonia hugged Noemie with an extra warm embrace. "You've been wonderful, hasn't she?"

I concurred, also embracing Noemie. "You've made our Paris trip really *exceptional*. It wouldn't have been the same without you."

Noemie smiled her eternal smile. "I've been so happy to have met you. You make an old lady think that all's well with the world after all."

"I'd like to write to you, to keep in touch with you," Sonia said, a damp gleam in her eyes.

"Yes, let's do that. Write to me about how you both are doing in far-away beautiful Miami. Send the letters here, to the bed-and-breakfast."

The next morning, true enough, Noemie had prepared a couple of sumptuous '*Croques Madame*' for our journey. We left the bed-and-breakfast, and strolled around the corner for one last walk down *Rue des Rosiers*. We had half-an-hour to kill before the cab would arrive to take us to the airport.

We saw Noemie's former restaurant, *Le Coq Qui Rit* and decided on the spur of the moment to go for one last *café au lait*. The place was half empty: it was still early, and the tourists hadn't yet arrived.

An older man, balding and polite, came to take our order. We ordered a couple of glasses of fresh-squeezed orange juice and two cups of coffee.

When he came back with the beverages, I out-of-the-blue asked him whether he knew Noemie.

"*Noemie*? The Noemie who used to own this restaurant?" he asked.

"Yes—*that* Noemie," I responded.

He looked at me, rolling his head downward slowly, as if apologizing. "Monsieur, I'm sorry to have to tell you this unfortunate news, but Noemie passed away about ten, maybe twelve years ago. I'm Jacques Hoffman—my wife Helene and I bought this restaurant from her well before she died…. Did you know her? She was a *wonderful* woman."

9

Siblings

*I*t *should have never been like this*, I told myself. When we finally met, I had tearfully, emotionally, told Jeannie, my one-and-only sister, that we should have grown up together. As it was, we were meeting for the first time in more than sixty-eight years.

Our story began many years ago, in an exotic country then called the Union of South Africa, at the southern end of the Dark Continent.

Our father had fortuitously arrived there just a few months before Austria had been speedily absorbed into Nazi Germany, as the newly-appointed second secretary of the Austrian Consulate.

His appointment came about due to a favor granted to *his* father, my grandfather, who was able to get *my* father into the *Diplomatenschule* at a time when Jews weren't allowed into Austria's Civil Service.

Because my father was Jewish, he was later unceremoniously fired by Hitler's Third Reich. He then pleaded with his now-Nazi diplomatic associates in Vienna to allow his fiancee to migrate to South Africa to join him there.

So it was that my mother hastily got married by proxy, marrying my uncle Frank, my father's older brother, in a rushed ceremony in Vienna, in order to be allowed out of Nazi-threatened Austria. She arrived in Cape Town, fearing for her extended family she had left behind, and in poor health, in early 1938.

I was born to a mother who would die of a cancerous thyroid and leave me, a seven-month-old infant, before the war in Europe broke out.

After my mother's tragic demise, my distraught father placed me in the loving care of my grandparents, his parents, who had somehow got out of Nazi-controlled Austria while the war was raging. My grandparents were in Johannesburg; my father continued working in Cape Town, one thousand miles away. My father would occasionally come up and visit us. By the time I was four, I was back in Cape Town; my father had remarried, and was managing Director of a hotel close to Cape Town's famed boardwalk, in the shadow of Table Mountain.

Little baby Jeannie, my sister, arrived about a year later. I remember that we lived in the hotel for a while. My stepmother hired a full-time nanny for my little sister. I recall that she was quiet and watchful, with large all-encompassing eyes. With her nanny, we used to take long walks in the afternoons, all the way to the docks.

Even though the four of us were living in a suite, my parents decided that it was too crowded. A short while later, we moved into a spacious two-story villa, built into a hill in Camps Bay, a sun-and-sea-washed Cape Town suburb. We occupied the second floor: our front door abutted the hill. To one side was a large monkey cage. The bottom floor, where the owners lived, had its front door facing the long sloping lawn, where a couple of peacocks majestically walked.

Jeannie was then about one year old, and I was approaching my seventh birthday. Our parents would sometimes, toward evening, place us either in the shade near the monkey cage, where we watched the cavorting carefree monkeys, or on the lawn observing the peacocks slowly preening themselves. Life was predictable and secure; sometimes we don't appreciate it while it lasts.

One Saturday morning, my father took me into town by bus. He pointed out certain landmarks along the way, and showed me how to handle small change for the bus ride. Once we were in downtown Cape Town, he gave me change for the return trip, plus money for a kid's movie show. I was only six year's old; I still wonder about his absolute belief that I'd be fine, that nothing untoward would happen to me.

Down the grassy slope of our villa's front garden, toward the coast road facing giant beachside rocks, the two peacocks set the tone for our bucolic tranquility. Some of the granite rocks close to the beach had huge holes in them, big enough for a small car to drive through. The coast road near the rocks was where I would wait for the bus to take me into town. Sometimes my stepmother would bring Jeannie in her stroller to see me off. I remember celebrating my seventh birthday on the seashore, together with a couple of friends. My stepmother packed a basket of goodies for me to take down to the beach.

The idyllic family life of my young years was irreparably shattered one Saturday morning, when I was seven and a couple of months old. I came back from my weekly trip to the movies to find my father in tears, hunched over his roll top desk.

"Daddy, what's wrong?" I asked him.

"Joy argued with me and took little Jeannie away with her."

"Where did they go?"

"I don't know."

"Will they come back?"

"I have no idea."

The ground under me started shaking. Or possibly it was my trembling legs.

The very next morning, I was taken to Cape Town's Central Railway Station and was put on a Johannesburg-bound train. My father came with me into the train compartment, and placed a large suitcase onto the rack above my head. Then he went down to the platform, reassuring me that my grandparents would be waiting for me at the station when the train arrived the next morning.

My heart was in my mouth. I couldn't believe that he was sending my on an overnight trip by myself. I clung onto the window hoping that somehow he would change his mind and come with me. He told me that I would be sleeping on the train, which would arrive in Johannesburg 'tomorrow.'

He explained that he had important things to take care of in Cape Town, but would be joining me 'in a short while.' I was very troubled, very nervous, thinking about being all alone for such a lengthy journey. He must have noticed, because he assured me that everything would be all right. I asked him about little Jeannie and my stepmother. He muttered something about having to take care of that situation as well.

As the train pulled away from the platform, I was joined in the compartment by a woman, a complete stranger. I sat stoically near the window, watching the suburbs gradually disappear, to be replaced by scrubland and rolling hills. The woman sat opposite me, looking through a magazine. After a while she asked me if I was travelling alone. Establishing that, she showed me where the bathroom was by taking me to the toilet. She even waited for me.

I had travelled by train before, and knew that the 'lavatories' were at the ends of cars, but this was the first time I had ever travelled overnight alone in my young life, and it was reassuring that she took an interest in me. Later, she told me it was time for lunch. I hesitated, not knowing what the procedure was. "Don't worry," she said, smiling. "Your meals were paid for when your father paid for the ticket. You can come with me to the dining car."

Time passed. After a fitful night, I was greeted by my doting grandparents at the station; they thanked the woman who had been so very kind to me. I told them what I knew about the events leading up to my hasty departure.

I lived with both my grandparents until my grandfather died when I was eight. My father was visiting us when that happened. It was wintertime in Johannesburg, and I remember that several people, including my father and grandmother were putting their coats on in preparation for going to visit my grandfather at the hospital. The phone rang; it was someone from the hospital, informing my grandmother that my '*Oupa*' had died.

After that deeply emotional shock, I continued living with my grandmother. I had turned eight. My father returned to Cape Town. He lied to us, weaving a tale of deception about Jeannie and my stepmother, telling my '*Ouma*' and me that he was in touch with them. My '*Ouma*' subsequently took me to the General

Post Office to mail her carefully wrapped wax-on-string birthday presents to my step-mother's family for little Jeannie; she never received them, because she wasn't there. Years later—many years later—I found out the truth about Jeannie's fate.

Sometime after my grandfather's death, my father moved to Johannesburg to be with his mother and me, joining her in the advertising business which my grandparents had founded. I was ecstatic to be living with him once again.

For a while all was well, but the whereabouts of my stepmother and little Jeannie continued to be a mystery. My father would tell us that my stepmother and Jeannie had gone back to stay with my stepmother's family, and refused to have any contact with him.

When I was not quite nine, I was sent to a sleep-away summer camp. My father used my absence to dupe my grandmother into a supposed meeting with him in downtown Johannesburg to discuss business. While she was out, he then doubled back to my grandmother's apartment to hastily grab items he thought belonged to him, and left for good. Upon my return from summer camp three days later, the apartment was still in a mess.

When my grandmother died two years later, my father was long gone. He completely disappeared; I never saw him again. I was then not quite eleven. My aunts and uncles in Johannesburg sold off my grandparents' possessions, and sent me to live with one of my father's brothers in England, my Uncle George.

Those were difficult years for me. My aunt made sure that I was under her thumb at all times, making my life miserable. She wanted me to know that I was not welcome there. For example, I was given margarine, whereas the rest of the family ate butter. Nonetheless, I studied hard; I had something to prove, to show her that I was worthy. I won a national writing award from a major daily newspaper. My biggest satisfaction in those doleful years was having a journalist and a photographer come to the house; I was written up as the first-prize winner. Seeing my aunt's dismayed reaction to my success was priceless.

Jeannie's fate was very different than mine, and in many respects, far more challenging and arduous. Unbelievably, she was returned to my father by Joy, her mother, probably a day or two after I had left Cape Town for Johannesburg. Obviously, I had no knowledge of her whereabouts at that time, or even many years later. Joy had decided that she didn't want little Jeannie any more. All of what follows is true; most of this comes from public records made available to me sixty-eight years later. To protect Jeannie, I'm leaving most of the lurid details out.

My father found a 'wet nurse' to take care of little Jeannie for a while. When that relationship came to an end, my father placed her in an orphanage. Evidently, he had misgivings about this, and pulled her out. Court records show that some time afterwards, he returned her to that establishment.

From there, she was adopted by a couple who later returned her to the same orphanage, citing some difficulties in fitting her in with their older children. All of this occurred while my father would come up to Johannesburg, assuring his parents and me that he was in touch with my sister and her mother.

Subsequently, Jeannie was adopted again. Her new adoptive mother turned out to be very abusive, but Jeannie somehow bravely weathered that storm.

When she graduated from high school, she enrolled in nursing school and became a nurse. She was working in a hospital where she met her future husband. They were married, and later had two daughters, my dear nieces. And together they lived a happy life.

My sister and her husband worked in their medical-related professions for a while. Eventually shunning city life, they moved to a farm which they had purchased because their two daughters loved horses.

(*It's interesting to note that on her farm Jeannie later took care of her once-abusive adoptive mother in that woman's dotage. In her senility, she completely changed her personality, and became meek and grateful for Jeannie's kindness.*)

By this time, I had left England and settled in Israel, where I continued my studies after serving in the Israeli Army. During that time, I was selected as one of the IDF's outstanding soldiers, and was decorated for bravery by Israel's then-President. I married my first wife there, and we welcomed our first child, a daughter. As a tank commander in the Sinai Desert, I played an important role in the Six-Day War.

All through those years of separation, I never forgot Jeannie. I put out feelers, trying to trace her, without success. It was as if she had completely vanished. I thought that she had emigrated, but I couldn't establish that.

A few more years went by. I had a Master's from Cornell by this time, and was working in Miami for a major accounting firm as their Management Advisor. I spent considerable periods on the road and overseas. I constantly thought about Jeannie, wondering where she was and what had happened to her; I had contacted the South African Embassy in Washington, DC for help, even asking fellow South African residents from Miami traveling to that country to see whether they could uncover a trace of her.

By now I was divorced, and for a while was single. I was absorbed by the quotidian grind of living, but always thought about how I could find my sister. She obviously didn't know of my existence, because when we were torn apart she was a one-year-old toddler. I was as far from finding her as ever. At that time, my younger daughter, a White House correspondent, used her connections to see whether she could find Jeannie through diplomatic channels. Nothing came of those efforts.

Things started becoming more promising with the advent of the computer age; I could get in touch with South African newspapers directly. They began publicizing my story, that I was searching for a long-lost sister.

My present wife Sonia and I decided on a trip to South Africa, to pick up the traces of Jeannie that were now tantalizingly close. I started getting offers of help from well-meaning locals. An amateur genealogist contacted me, and offered her services. Things were finally churning.

Arriving in Jo'burg, we checked into a charming bed-and-breakfast guest house, and were visited by the genealogist. She told us that she had made contact with the adoption agency which had handled Jeannie's two adoptions. Evidently, she had authorized the agency, two short years before, to grant access to her records, since she was also trying to trace her biological parents. The genealogist said that she would hear from Jeannie in a matter of days.

My wife and I were scheduled to leave for Cape Town, the city where Jeannie and I had lived in our formative years. Once we arrived there, we rushed to a cyber-café, and placed a fateful call. The genealogist had done what she had promised; contact had been made.

Excited, we cut short our visit to Cape Town. We flew back to Jo'burg. We had found out that Jeannie was living on a farm with her husband and one of her two daughters; the other daughter lived in the city, and had a daughter, my grandniece.

The very next day, we scheduled a meeting with one of my newly-discovered nieces at the hotel where she worked. When we met, she kissed me full on my lips, as all close relatives do. She drove us to the farm, where I had a long-overdue, emotional reunion with my kid sister, sixty-eight years after we last saw one another. I will always remember our joy at being reunited.

I've since been back. And like most siblings do, worldwide, we're in regular touch. Now that we've reconnected, Jeannie is an important part of my life. Better late than never at all.

10

Stranded in a Foreign Land

When he got to their agreed-upon meeting place, three fat logs arranged in a triangle close to the water, John White saw just two of his Assistants awaiting him; most of the others, evidently, were still wrapping up their chores.

He nodded to the two, who assured him that the others were on their way. John White was a man of patience, at peace with nature and gentle with all manner of people, as befitted a leader of men who was the appointed Governor of the colony; he was also a talented painter and watercolorist.

He had brought his pregnant daughter and son-in-law with him this time, and other family members as well. In fact, he had selected and assembled his diverse group of colonists almost single-handedly. Having Sir Walter Raleigh as sponsor and protector of the group was also a powerful persuader.

Once people in London found out what White was planning to do, the intriguing and appealing concept of colonizing the

New World was captivating to many; a significant number of people were disenchanted with the direction society was taking. On many levels, the population was rebelling against the blatant and ever-growing excesses and corruption of the two competing Churches, as well as the debased elitist cultural scatology of the ruling classes. In addition, prospective settlers considering emigration to the New World were being promised five hundred acres of land; this last was of particular interest to adventuresome, free-thinking individuals who were actively seeking a better, more meaningful life than what they endured in over-crowded, crime-ridden and polluted London and other cities.

"Methinks it'll take a little while longer to rebuild the abandoned fort by following the entrenchments we found," said Richard Taverner, a burly man who could be counted on to do his fair share of chopping down trees and hauling trunks and branches.

White concurred. "*True*, Richard, but we have double duty to perform. *Both* are important; we also have to rebuild the houses that were demolished. Our families need living space as well."

Thomas Harris interjected. He was a former Cambridge professor, one of several former academics who had opted for the New World. "We'll feel a whole lot better about our colony once we move into our own homes, that's for certain."

John White sat down. "And what do you think of the fort?"

Richard Taverner looked in the direction of the logs, one piled on top of another. "Quite large and quite defensible. A fair-sized stronghold... roughly square in dimension, with pinched corners."

White smiled. "Those, according to military men, are called 'bastions,' to better defend the fort in the event that it's attacked."

"That obviously happened — to the fort, I mean," Harris said.

"The soldiers must have been overrun by the Red Indians — *they* surely did this dastardly deed. They looked upon the soldiers as invaders, and killed them all," observed Taverner.

John White shrugged. "I don't know... there's always the possibility that they fled. What happened to them after they left, no-one knows."

"And then there's the mystery of the one soldier who died. Maybe the Indians left his bones as a warning to us, or anyone else who thought about colonizing this place."

John White agreed. "I'm sure that it was some kind of sign.... This place looked deserted, the moment we set foot on land, right from the start."

At that point, most of White's remaining Assistants, with the exception of Master Pilot Simon Fernandez and two others, joined the original three sitting on the logs; there were now nine of the twelve Assistants present.

John White sighed heavily. "Welcome, everyone. How are the repairs going?"

Ananias Dare, who was John White's son-in-law, voiced the sentiments of most. "We're slowly repairing the damage, clearing away the debris. There's much to be done."

"How's Eleanor doing?"

Ananias thought about his very pregnant wife, White's daughter. "She's suffering, poor dear. The heat, you know. I constructed a soft chair, almost a bed, and placed it under that large yew tree near our house, presently under construction."

White nodded, visualizing his daughter; he planned to sit with her after the Assistants' meeting. "And how is Margery Harvie doing? Also suffering, no doubt."

"Aye. According to Dyonis, she'll give birth shortly, probably just after Eleanor."

"Good, good...." John White looked each of his Assistants in the eyes, wanting to impress upon them the precarious nature of their situation.

"All of this is very troubling to me. For those of you who know me well, I don't need to explain how much we depend on friendly relations with our neighbors, the Secotan and Croatoan Indians."

"John—what's the situation exactly, between us and the Indians?"

John White was not at all upset about not being addressed as 'Governor.' In fact, he encouraged members of his colony to treat one another as absolute equals.

"No single one of us is in any way superior or more important than any other in our colony," he would say, and others would nod their agreement. After all, that was one of the major reasons why his group had come to this isolated spot. They considered themselves '*separatists*'; they had become disenchanted with what was going on in England from a cultural, political and religious standpoint. They especially decried the elevation of clergy and all differences of rank among people.

"I'm very worried about what has happened between us and the Croatoans…. They had very good reason to expel the soldiers, based on what happened the last time I was here…. This is a vast and unexplored wilderness. We have only just begun to map the coastline. Who knows what lies beyond the local tribal lands."

"You've only told us snippets of what really happened," said Christopher Cooper. "Why did the Indians forcefully expel the soldiers and completely destroy the fort? I think that we have a right to know, because it's our lives that hang in the balance."

John White retorted. "You're right, Christopher. I'll start from the beginning…. Our troops were led by a certain Captain Ralph Lane." He looked around at his Assistants. "Some of you may know of him. He learned his strong-arm tactics in Ireland, and he decided to treat the Indians as if they were dirt as well. He's a brutal man, who would rather *kill* than negotiate…. When he came here last time, a couple of years ago, to Roanoke, he laid waste one of the Indian's major settlements, and burned whole fields of corn which the Croatoans were counting on to survive the winter."

"Why would he provoke the Indians instead of coexisting with them?"

White retorted. "As I said, he's a narrow-minded brute. Would you *believe* — it was all because a silver cup went missing. Captain Lane wanted to teach them a lesson, not to meddle with the white man, *Englishmen* specifically. He accused the Croatoans of stealing the cup, and all hell broke loose."

"Why would he do such a thing?"

White spoke in a choked voice, remembering the occasion. "Lane was in charge of the troops. We were the guests of the local Indian leader, Wingina. He was their king. Wingina's wife, too, was very regal. The Indians venerated them both."

"And what happened?"

"We were in Secota, their most important town. We'd enjoyed a day of feasting and merrymaking together with the locals. We'd come there after trading and feasting in another of their towns.

"We had brought along some fine examples of goods: clothing and various manufactured wares from home. They were dazzled by our products. Everything was laid out on mats for them to examine. They had also laid out mats, which were loaded with pots and plates of cooked foods, meats, fish, and platters of fresh vegetables. Some of their foods were unknown to us, grown and raised here in the New World. For example, the tall stalks of corn-on-the-cob, and those magnificent giant sunflowers. We were amazed at the variety of what they showed us.

"Some of their women were dishing out the food, laughing and smiling. Everyone was trading, bartering, eating and having a good time.

"One of our traders had given a little doll to King Wingina's pretty little daughter. She must have been nine or ten. She was proudly holding a doll manufactured in London, so very far away. I even sketched a picture of her and presented it to King Wingina; he was wide-eyed with wonder at my exact depiction of his pretty, dark-eyed daughter. That day, I sketched lots of other sketches of their town, which I took back with me to England."

"And then this Captain Lane was informed that the cup was missing."

"Exactly. We had established a genuine friendship with King Wingina and his tribe. I could envision cooperation and mutual assistance, so that our coming here would be made easier, so that there'd be a lasting peace between us —"

"Then this Captain Lane was enraged about the loss of that silver cup, and so didn't take into account all the good will and friendship between the two peoples?"

"As I said, he's a brute, who doesn't give any quarter. He wanted to show them that Englishmen cannot be trifled with."

"So that's why the Indians didn't show their faces when we arrived."

"Yes. All of you know Manteo from the journey over here. He's one of them, a Croatoan, even though he's now dressed in fine London clothing, as fine as any we wear. Manteo told me that they're *very* angry at us, and blame us for the harsh winter which they had to endure without the usual food reserves."

"How does he know that they're angry?"

White looked steadily at the Assistant who asked the question; he was Ananias Dare, his son-in-law. "Ananias, Manteo knows how the Croatoans think. If King Wingina is opposed to making a peaceful gesture, the whole Croatoan nation won't come to the shore to greet us. Manteo thinks that possibly *I* could convince Wingina to have a peace conference."

"So are you going to go to the King's town in order to plead with him?"

"Yes—I think that it's absolutely necessary. We should go as a delegation to Wingina and humbly apologize for what our soldiers did."

Several of the Assistants spoke simultaneously.

John Jones, the colony's physician spoke over the cacophony of voices. "Were the fort and the houses complete the last time you were here?"

"Yes—that was one of the only good things Captain Lane accomplished. He lasted a whole winter before going home, leaving fifteen soldiers behind to man the fort until supply ships arrived from England."

"Aye," agreed Christopher Cooper. "And the Indians really broke it up. They didn't leave two logs one on top of t'other."

White got up, and began pacing between the triangular arrangement of the logs. "For them, the fort and our little houses were *defiled*, unclean... *polluted*. They wanted to return the land to what it was before the English appeared here."

"What do you think we can do to repair our relationship with the Indians?"

John White stuck his chin out defiantly. "I'm going to appeal to King Wingina. He probably is still mourning the passing of his brother Granganimeo, who died while we were still here. He died from 'white man's disease.' In reality, lots of Croatoans mysteriously died. Maybe it was due to a comet that we all saw in the night sky, a portend for a terrible disaster. On the other hand, possibly we *unknowingly* brought in the disease when we arrived here.

"But Wingina knows me as a man of peace. I presented personal sketches to him and his wife as a token of brotherhood between us, and a sign that I held them in high esteem. Manteo, who is helping to build one of the homes which was partially destroyed and overgrown with weeds, will translate for me.

"Do you think that this Captain Lane will be back here when the supply ships arrive?"

"No, I believe that his North American service is done, finished. I reported his actions to Walter Raleigh, so that he could inform everyone at Court, including the Queen. Captain Lane's no longer welcome here because of the damage and destruction he has caused."

Suddenly, two men ran toward the clearing, their muskets held aloft with the cadence of their hurried gait; they were the missing Assistants.

The other men sitting waiting for their arrival saw the panic in their eyes.

"*They killed poor George Howe* — the Indians killed George Howe!" Anthony Cage gasped out the words as he huffed for breath, spewing phlegm.

John White, so shocked that he leaped upright from where he was sitting, uttered "How?"

"Where? Where did this happen?" John Jones asked.

"A couple of miles from here," panted the other arriving Assistant, John Chapman, trying to catch his breath. "He must have wandered away from the rest of us…. We were out looking for crabs, since our food supply is so precarious…. Poor George was almost nude save for some skivvies, with nothing but a cloth sling to carry the crabs and a forked stick…. We found him face down in shallow water, with *sixteen* arrows in him. They really *meant* to kill him. And then for good measure, they also bashed in his head, probably with clubs…. Poor George… and his son George Junior here in camp, waiting for his father."

John White stroked his beard. He was the appointed Governor of the group; he realized that his colony of one hundred seventeen newly arrived settlers was in dire trouble. "*Find me Manteo. We need him to help us smooth things over with the Croatoan Indians, or there will be hell to pay.*"

John White and Manteo led a delegation of Assistants through the packed sand and scrubland, across a stretch of soft pine needles underfoot, down into the dense woodland with Spanish moss dripping from the serried canopy overhead, which at times blotted out the light, and through to an area of sharp sawgrass. The forward motion of their feet becomes sticky, damp and knotty.

They pass by a cardamom forest of towering trees; some noisy parrots chatter and squawk, breaking the silence around them.

Manteo leads them around a reed-filled estuary, past some sand islands. Somewhere close by a whippoorwill's mating call echoes off some adjacent cypress trees. A lone heron spreads her long wings and gracefully takes flight; they can hear the rhythmic beating of its wings as it gains height.

"They watch us, see all over," Manteo says to White.

White keeps his head down, but anxiously scans the surrounding trees and reeds for any sign of Indians. "You know that for sure, right?"

"I sure. I know my brothers."

They plod on; John White looks back every so often to make certain that his group is intact.

They reach Secota, Wingina's capital. Long houses with arched roofs, to the left and right, line a wide central avenue, which ends in front of a final long house. Around the town are fields of tall green corn stalks and huge sunflowers; White is the only settler to have seen and admired these before.

He leads his delegation straight up the central avenue, aware that many pairs of eyes are upon them. The population of the town is seated in a horseshoe configuration, open to the approaching visitors. Wingina and his wife are seated together in a prominent position in the front of the center of the horseshoe.

"Wingina know we come," said Manteo, unnecessarily.

The delegation of settlers approached Wingina, who remained stoically silent. Once he was in front of the king, White bowed his head in deference; Wingina nodded slowly. "Manteo, introduce yourself to King Wingina."

Manteo did so, and brought a broad smile of recognition from the king. They had a lengthy conversation in the Croatoan language. The king gestured to several of the people seated immediately behind him, some of whom rose to hug and greet Manteo.

White reached into his leather jerkin, and pulled out a beaten copper paneled choker, and a filigreed gilt-metal necklace set with glass stones. He held them toward Wingina, and nodded to Manteo. "Tell the king that these are our gifts of appreciation and hope that we can return to the mutual love and respect which our two peoples had, before our troops went wild. Tell the king that we wish to apologize for the terrible things done to the peaceful Croatoan nation."

Manteo went through the explanation.

Wingina remained unmoved; White tried to get a reaction from him. "Tell the king that we have lost too many good people on both sides, some very close to us. It is time now for peace, and to stop killing innocent people."

Manteo translated; Wingina pursed his lips and listened closely. Once Manteo had finished, White noticed that Manteo backed away, cast his eyes downward and placed his hands together in a deferential pose. Wingina remained silent.

John White grew edgy; Wingina's silence wasn't a good indication. Finally he spoke, his voice reedy and choked.

John White looked at Manteo, still with his eyes downcast. Eventually Manteo spoke, so quietly that White had to lean forward to hear him.

"King Wingina say no to gifts. He no accept. People suffered... many... died because of white man."

White put the gifts carefully into his jerkin; from the other side, he pulled out a picture book. "Tell King Wingina this is for his daughter... a book of doll pictures and doll houses which I'm sure she'll love to see. In appreciation from me."

Manteo translated. After some hesitation, Wingina reached for the book and immediately gave it to his wife, seated beside him. She smiled a shy smile, looking down at the book cover on her lap. Her little ten-year-old daughter sat beside her mother, unmoving.

White was determined to make something of his small victory in Wingina accepting a token on behalf of his daughter. "Tell King Wingina that I'd like to invite him to a peace celebration at Roanoke."

White watched as Manteo spoke to Wingina. When Manteo had finished, Wingina launched into a lengthy speech. White saw flashes of anger in the king's eyes.

Manteo nodded, looking down at the ground when Wingina had finished. "King Wingina say no food for white man. Winter coming. Not enough food to share. Also, he to talk… *discuss* … with other tribes first. He say if other kings agree, he will bring other kings with… but not before seven days. He must discuss first."

John White bowed. "Tell King Wingina that we will await his arrival with the other kings in seven days. Tell him that we are grateful, and that I want us, our two people, to be friends like before."

Manteo spoke slowly to the king. When he had finished, Manteo backed away, looking down. The king nodded, and stood up: the whole tribe stood up with him. Apart from the barking of the tribes' dogs, and some geese honking overhead, everything was silent.

"We go now," said Manteo.

One week went by quickly. Considerable progress had been made in the reconstruction of the fort, as well as the small cabins. Guards were now posted on the outskirts of the growing settlement, as a precaution against surprise Indian raids. No Indians were seen; it was as if they were avoiding the settlers completely.

On the eighth day since the meeting with Wingina, White got his Assistants together by the triangular logs. He had summoned them there with a heavy heart. "We can't expect any peaceful coexistence with the Croatoans, nor with the Secotans, who also are in our neighborhood."

He looked around for any reaction; everyone was there, apart from Simon Fernandez, the pilot who had brought them to Roanoke, even though the original destination had been the far more promising Chesapeake Bay area. Fernandez had used every ploy in order to complicate their arrival, and had now refused to take them any further.

"I have pleaded with Pilot Fernandez to take us to Chesapeake from here, but he says that it's too late in the season to move. Besides, our cabins are almost built. So we'll stay here, at least for the winter."

"Wouldn't we have a better situation at Chesapeake, since the Indians there would hopefully be friendlier, even though it's late in the season?"

"Correct, we would. But Master Pilot Fernandez has set us here instead, for his own devious reasons. So we will stay here, and pray that we survive the winter."

A couple of weeks later, the colony celebrated the birth of Virginia Dare, John White's granddaughter. For a short time of sheer bliss, everyone forgot their precarious foodstuffs and provisions situation.

Two weeks and a few days later, Margery Harvie gave birth to a son. After the celebrating, John White once again called his Assistants to their triangular meeting place.

Once they were all seated, White ripped a bough off of the log he was sitting on, and used it to push down into his left boot. "An itch in an unreachable place," he noted dryly. "Which reminds me of something we have to do."

"What is that?" asked Richard Wildye.

"One of us has to go back to England with Pilot Fernandez, in order to plead our case, and our cause…. That's perfectly obvious, because if supply ships come in this direction, they're going to try to find us in the Chesapeake Bay area, and not here. Fernandez is obviously doing the bidding of someone of authority who wants our group to fail."

Christopher Cooper spoke up. "What *proof* do you have of that, John? And if true, who better to go back than *you*? You have easy access to Walter Raleigh, who has the Queen's ear on all matters of interest."

"I'll give you not just *one* proof of his deceitfulness, I'll remind you of the nine, or *ten* proofs. But first I have to remind you, since I'm the appointed Governor, that my place is *here*."

William Browne frowned. "I believe that you are the best spokesman for the colony, John—you and nobody else."

White demurred. "I'm reminded of Will Shakespeare and the Globe Theatre. You all know of him, right? Well, according to Walter Raleigh, Shakespeare merely *produces* and acts in his plays. He's never traveled out of England, so how could poor, semi-educated Will write so knowingly about deep cultural entanglements and historic perfidies in Continental Europe? The *real* author and creative genius is the Earl of Oxford. When the Earl's not touring all over Europe, he's at the Queens' Court, always in her entourage....

"And if the educated and sophisticated Earl was writing this script—*our script*—it would be a *tragedy* he'd be writing. But because he is a Lord and likes to stay in the background and not sully his name, it's *Shakespeare* who is his chosen messenger, *Shakespeare* who gets the acclaim.

"I'm like the Earl—I'll stay at home—*here*—this is my Court. And I'll pass the responsibility of going back to one of you."

The Assistants looked at one another, as if deciding who the emissary would be, if not John White. They were silent.

"I'm going to pick one of you, if you can't make up your minds." White looked around the faces of his Assistants, sizing each one up. Upon not seeing anyone willing to volunteer, he adjudged. "I've decided," he finally stated. "*Christopher*—you are my choice to go and fight for our colony in England.... *Don't object*—my mind's made up."

Christopher Cooper resisted. 'John, I believe that this is a mistake on your part. I wouldn't know *how* to put our argument forward. *You* could do a lot better."

White reached into his jerkin and pulled out ten scraps of paper, one after the other. "We're going to play a game here. Actually *not* a game, but a learning tool. This tool is going to be used by the one who's going back to England."

He looked around. "I sincerely hope that all of us come through this experience alive. But if all of us don't -" he waved the scraps of paper— "I want as *many* of you as possible to remember how we arrived in this godforsaken place, thanks to the obvious perfidy and treachery of our Pilot, Simon Fernandez. We have to give this information to Walter Raleigh, so that he can speak to the Queen about these acts of sabotage."

White walked around the triangle, handing out the scraps of paper. Once done, he sat down and pulled out a bigger piece of paper. "All the scraps have a number on them. Last night I documented *ten* acts of deliberate deceit and deception, including a couple which could have been accidental, and therefore forgivable. But remember that Master Pilot Simon Fernandez was trained in the finest pilots' school in the world, and knows the islands of the New World and the coastline of these parts *intimately*…. He's supposed to know where things are, and where to go to get them. Like the back of his own hand."

White looked around. "All right, let's begin: who has Number One?"

Thomas Hewer raised his hand.

"Thomas, in the Assizes, in the courts of law back home, you as a lawyer wouldn't be able to deny that Master Pilot Fernandez didn't *deliberately* leave our Flyboat behind in dangerous Portuguese waters when we were on our way here. He was hoping never to see it again, but he was very disappointed. That's an act of *sabotage*. That's Number One."

White rolled his pointer finger back and forth opposite the faces of his Assistants. "Number Two?"

Richard Wildye acknowledged.

"Richard, you will agree with me that when Pilot Fernandez brought us to Santa Cruz, he promised us abundant water and sheep. Not only did he *lie*, but I later found shards and pieces of pottery on the island, after he had assured us that the island was not inhabited. He exposed us to danger... we could have been attacked.... Number Three!"

"William.... Pilot Fernandez sent Captain Stafford in our third ship, the little pinnace, to Beak Island, promising him that he would find needed salt and fresh water there: there was absolutely none...."

"*Four*—who has Four?"

Ananias Dare raised a finger.

"Ah, my dear son-in-law…. Pilot Fernandez arrives in Hispaniola waters, but without explanation, doesn't land there. By this time, obviously, our two ships are *putrid*: we should have at least cleaned our galleys and taken on water. But, no—he refuses…. Number Five!

"Ah, John, Doctor John…. Three days later, Pilot Fernandez takes us to Caicos and promises us salt, but there is none there. Without salt we can't preserve our meat. *Next*!

"Number Six—*Ambrose*: nine days later, Pilot Fernandez thinks that he's arrived at Croatoan, but he's wrong. We waste a couple of days, and he doesn't even bother to consult Manteo, who knows his own lands *intimately*…. Number Seven.

"Thomas… good reliable Thomas…. Captain Stafford saves Pilot Fernandez from running into Cape Fear… that would have meant the end for most of us. Our biggest and best ship, the 'Lion,' would have broken up and sunk with all aboard…. Number Eight!

"Our Flyboat, with Captain Spicer guiding her, miraculously finds us once we have arrived. Spicer had never been here before. Once Fernandez sees Spicer's ship, which Fernandez sailed away from while in Portuguese waters, he becomes extremely angry and upset…. Number Nine.

"*Nine*…Pilot Fernandez refused to take us on to Chesapeake, where the Indians haven't had any bad experiences with white men, and our likelihood of living in peace with them are much more likely than here. In addition, he claims that it's too late in the season, but he's been dawdling here for *thirty-six* days!"

"And Number Ten?" someone asked.

"Ah, yes, *Number Ten....* Only *one* of us, he says, can return to England with the three ships. Whoever goes will sail with Captain Spicer on the Flyboat. Fernandez is going to be home much quicker—he'll make certain of that—so that he can tell everyone all the way up to the Queen what a success the voyage was."

"What will become of us?" John Jones, the colony's physician enquired.

"I don't know. Without supply ships knowing where we are, we have to somehow survive this coming winter. As it is, we aren't a high priority, since the Queen insists on fealty to the Anglican Church. We are neither Church of England nor Roman Catholic. She would prefer that we remove ourselves from her Realm, unless we agree to return to her fold. Separatists like us are neither fish nor fowl. We have no friends, apart from one another."

◈

The following day, John White is informed that the Assistants are unanimous: they all petition that he, John White, return to England in order to plead their case, He grudgingly accepts.

He has an emotional parting from his daughter, his son-in-law and from little Virginia, his infant granddaughter. On board Captain Spicer's Flyboat, he watches as slowly, his daughter Eleanor disappears from view. His colony is stranded in a foreign land….

By the time he arrives in London, England is still gripped with the fear of a delayed Spanish invasion. He tries desperately to get back to his colony as soon as he is able; when he eventually does, it is too late. No one is there to greet him.

The colony on Roanoke Island is doomed, forfeited by circumstance. Although he and many others over the years diligently search for a trace, no European ever sees anyone from the Lost Colony again.

In modern times, the ability to explore the intricate traces of sixteenth century intrigue and deceit is difficult, in spite of the wealth of information we have accumulated.

Sir Walter Raleigh rose from obscurity to become Queen Elizabeth's constant companion and Court favorite. His sudden rise to great influence made him vulnerable to attack. He was known to be a defender and promoter of 'separatists,' which exposed him to those in high positions in Court who were forever plotting his downfall. Years after Elizabeth's death, he is hanged for committing treason. The Spanish celebrate; their great nemesis has finally been eliminated.

Twenty years after Roanoke, Jamestown on the Chesapeake Bay will be founded; thirteen years later, the Mayflower drops anchor off Plymouth Rock. Both of these groups are Separatists.

England has joined their European competitors in colonizing the New World; the age of exploration has begun in earnest.

11

The Crusader

Lucan was tired. Sweat filled his tunic and his riding pants. Droplets of perspiration ran down his face and into his eyes. His steel helmet baked in the unforgiving sun; his head felt as if he had placed it in an oven. His nosepiece added to his discomfort. He wrestled a heavy mailed glove off to flick the sweat off of his brow. His back ached. He felt like calling a rest break and dismounting, but there were no sheltering trees in the immediate area, only scrubland, patches of dried-out weeds and occasional bushes. He cast a glance at his troops riding behind him. His eyes settled on Percival, his loyal sergeant-at-arms. Percival was a horse's length from him, ever watchful, looking for any impending danger.

Since leaving the bustling port of Acre and the powerful fleet assembled there, Lucan's mounted force had encountered no one of any military significance. A few leagues out of the lively and ever-growing Crusader port city, they had run into a long caravan of merchants, with their goods piled high on stately camels.

A little further out, as the sun rose higher into the steamy sky, they passed a couple of *khirbehs*, ruins of ancient crumbling settlements, half-buried in the sand which seemed to cloak everything, blowing in one direction, and then another.

Percival shouted to draw his attention; Lucan followed his pointed finger and saw an approaching dust storm looming, angry and threatening, blowing in from the horizon. Lucan had been warned about the *Khamsin,* hot desert storms which blew mercilessly with the searing heat of an oven, sometimes for days on end, driving sane men into delirium. "We'd best be hunkering down somewhere safe."

Lucan rose up on his stirrups and saw a *khirbeh* not far from where they were riding.

"Let's head there." He whistled shrilly and pointed in the slight change of direction.

On the way there, leading his large group of mounted soldiers, he looked down at the parched ground, reflecting on what had brought him to this desolate place.

His over-active mind drew lightning-fast flashbacks, like fiery particles being ignited in his brain. He thought about his father, Prince Johannes, who had left him, as a ten-year-old, in the care of his mother while he went off on a Crusade. The Crusade was successful: the Crusader Knights had strengthened the Christian Kingdom of Jerusalem, building more strategic forts and castles to foil the repeated Saracen attempts to recapture the Holy City. But his father had died a violent death in the effort, unwittingly leading his soldiers into a trap set by the wily Saracens.

One of the results of this unsettling and tragic occurrence in Lucan's early life was that he was frequently visited at night by dreams of his father, especially when Lucan was pondering on which course of action to take before a difficult choice. As he grew into adulthood, he continued to have nocturnal visits.

This is working out quite well, he thought. *Father is advising me, and so far he's never been wrong.*

Lucan found himself looking forward to his father's spectral visits. His father's ghost had boldly come to his bedside, and had whispered advice directly in his ear.

One night several months before, when Lucan was contemplating setting a date for his marriage to his betrothed, his father's ghost came to him in a dream.

"Son, I advise you to postpone your nuptials…. There are more important things you should do. My bones are scattered in the Holy Land, the place toward which our prayers are directed, and where our Savior lived and breathed. I have no marker for you to shed a tear over for the memory of me, no gravestone above my bones for you to visit and pray over. My remains will get no small comfort from your softly treading feet above them as you respectfully seek some of my earthly remains.

"But more importantly, our cause there is still in grave danger of failing. The enemy is constantly searching for signs of weakness on our side. They know that our soldiers are commanded by princes and dukes from different lands, and they try to take advantage of any perceptible chinks in out armor.

"So therefore, my dear son, I beseech you: you *must* become a Holy Crusader before you settle into married life. You can leave the running of the Principality to your mother, just as it was after I had left for the Holy Land, never to return. Do not forget, and do not disappoint me."

Lucan remembered that he had awoken, refreshed. It was as if his father's advice had removed mental impediments from his life's path.

Lucan's thoughts then flitted to his betrothed, Mathilde, who had been 'recommended' to him by his advisors and chancellors, because the marriage would expand his family's land holdings. He hadn't yet seen her and talked with her, but he had received a flattering mini-portrait of her, and had arranged a meeting between the two families.

When Lucan had first met Mathilde, he had liked her. She wasn't exactly the beauty as depicted in the small portrait, but she was graceful and feminine; after all she was a Hohenstauffen princess.

Lucan found her to be more desirable and appealing than almost all the women that he had bedded, who were mostly easily-enticed, willing chambermaids, with the occasional knight's daughter for variety. As the dashing young heir to his father's holdings, he had had easy options when it came to whom to bed. He had found out that there was stiff competition for his favors among the female courtiers and retainers in the palace. Being his bedmate elevated the status of Lucan's choice of the moment. He had merely to beckon with a finger and his sexual wish was fulfilled.

Lucan's advisors felt that it was time for him to wed and accept the responsibilities of his status. Lucan's father's ghost visited him again on the night after he had decided to wed. His father had appeared, almost on demand, to allay any further doubts Lucan may have had about his pending course of action.

During that night, Lucan recalled that he had felt a tremendous heaviness on his torso, so massive and complete that he couldn't move. Even his eyes were leaden. Lucan's father's ghost had appeared, slowly making his way to the side of Lucan's bed. He actually felt his father's warm breath on his ear. His voice echoed and re-echoed in his brain long after the dream had run its course. *"Go to the Holy Land, son. Your fate will be sealed there,*

*and you will be a Man, unchallenged in your glory. Your subjects will
look up to you as a god, a hero."*

Lucan was seriously thinking about his father's advice. Then, as
fate would have it, a chance visit to his castle by an older knight
who was passing through really sealed Lucan's fate.

The knight, himself a former Crusader, told Lucan that he absolutely had to embark on the Crusade, which was then being orga-
nized, before he should marry Mathilde, to initiate himself into
responsible manhood as the leader of the combined principalities.

What a coincidence, Lucan thought. *It's almost a conspiracy. The
fates want me to go. I'm being tempted.*

"If you stay, My Liege," said the elderly knight, "you will forever
regret not going in glory's quest. And if you go, you will be an
acclaimed Crusader, a leader of men, a man who challenged fate,
a prince of men who looked for and possibly found the Holy Grail,
or our Lord Jesus' crown of thorns. The prestige and honor will
be yours forever, for as long as you live."

Heeding his father's and the knight's advice, Lucan traveled to
the nearby Hohenstaufen principality to explain himself to his
betrothed, Mathilde. He was unsure whether his betrothed would
agree with his decision. He used his ghostly father's reasoning,
explaining that he was leaving on a Crusade to the Holy Land in
order to achieve glory and to prove himself worthy of marrying

her. She dutifully and reluctantly accepted his decision, asking him only that he come back safely to her.

He then told his mother about his decision. She had looked at him long and hard, with her piercing gaze. "Are you sure about this, son? What is the reason for your wanting to became a knight Crusader? Is it because you want to avenge your dear father's death, or is it something else?"

He had come up with his reasoning. His mother had looked at the floor and had nodded slightly; she knew that it was useless to argue with her son.

All of these thoughts and recollections flashed through Lucan's brain at lightning speed as he returned to the present moment. He immediately became aware of his discomfort, but allowed his faithful horse to carry him forward as he sank back into his reveries, continuing to ponder and lucubrate about his recent past actions.

Once he had made up his mind to leave and lead a group of mounted soldiers whom he had recruited, paid for, and trained, he had joined a group of knights who had decided like him to go to the Holy Land on the latest sacred Crusade. Duke Rupert of Augsburg, who had been on the previous Crusade, had invited the prospective Crusaders to his *schloss* high on a mountaintop.

The good Duke had been selected by the ruling organizers of the upcoming Crusade to explain to the group what exactly they could expect on the voyage and what awaited them in the bitterly contested and mysterious Holy Land.

The group of forty Knight-Crusaders from various parts of the Holy Roman Empire of German States were seated in various chairs scattered around a long table still laden with food and drink after a sumptuous dinner. The large room was well lit by flaming torches of tallow; the torches flickered and the greasy smoke wove slowly in circles before settling low to the floor.

The Duke spoke slowly, deliberately. "Tonight I will tell you truths and revelations about your journey, and about what awaits you once you arrive. Most of you have fluency in Upper German, which I will use tonight. I will also use some Latin, which may help those of you from other regions.

"You have to be aware that challenges will be everywhere, right from the start. On board ship, make certain that your men drink plenty of potable water, from unpolluted sources. Take plenty of barrels on board, enough for your men for a ten-day sea voyage, twelve if possible. Spare no expense. Remember, '*nervos belli, pecuniam infinitam.*' Your men will appreciate good food, and lots of it. And remember to pay them on time.

"Your horses *can* drink brackish water, as you well know, but they too would *appreciate* a plentiful supply of good clean water. It's hot down there in the ships' holds. Plenty of fresh hay as well.

Make sure every second day to brush and clean and wash them. They, like you, will be in an environment strange to their sensitivities. "It will be hotter than Hades, with humidity stickier than porridge. There are snakes thicker than a man's forearm, and scorpions too. I also have to mention exotic ticks and strange insects that you will have to contend with. And then of course there are the Saracens."

There was some nervous laughter around the large room. The Duke looked around, noting that all eyes were on him. "You will encounter the enemy, the heathen Saracens. I'll come around to them shortly. But first let me tell you about the flies… yes, the flies. There's a standing joke over there about the flies, especially those blasted horseflies. They are the size of a man's thumb below the knuckle. At least they appear to be, the larger ones. The joke is that you have to fight the damned creature for that bite-sized piece of meat lying on your plate If you look away from it, it'll be gone."

There were belly-laughs and guffaws from his audience of knights.

"I'm serious: they're not quite as bad as I describe, but be aware." He shifted to another subject.

"Acre is our major port in the Holy Land. It is lively, with our Crusader ships laden with supplies and fighting men coming and going constantly.

"Once you arrive, get your men and especially your horses accustomed to dry land once again. Practice cantering, and then galloping. Get your soldiers to practice plenty of hand-to-hand combat, on foot as well as when mounted.

"If we display our superior sword-play, we will win the day. *Be bold, be brash*—that's how we will best our enemy, those filthy heathen Saracens.

"Once you've engaged them, be careful of their *traps*—they are masters of deceit, of galloping away, as if they've broken and run. This is one of their great tactics, a wonderful deception.

"I was dragged into one of their '*fight, then suddenly flee*' battles. We gave chase, and immediately found that we'd been led into a beautifully disguised trap. They surrounded us, hacking away at us from all sides. We were overwhelmed, and I was lucky to escape with my life."

Duke Rupert looked around, making eye contact with Lucan.

"Prince Lucan of the Burgundian Lands knows full well of what I speak. His honorable father, Prince Johannes, died in a battle similar to what I just described. May he be remembered for his sacrifice, and may his memory protect you on your Crusade.... I want to show you a souvenir from the Holy Land, to remind you of what I speak."

He smiled wryly, and unbuttoned his shirt; he fingering a scar which ran down his left cheek and continued onto his shoulder.

"As I said, the Saracens almost succeeded in doing away with me as well, almost cutting off my head; if it were not for some protection around my neck.... I can see the turbaned Devil now, in my mind's eye, as he hacked at me with his flashing scimitar.... Don't get duped into chasing them—you'll die if you do."

He looked around slowly. "Remember, *dulce et decorum est pro patria mori*. But heroic sacrifice can also be a terrible waste, if you lay down your life needlessly, stupidly. Don't give up your life cheaply—it's the only one you have."

Prince Rupert sipped a glass of mead at his side. "A couple of more details. Beware of the weather, especially during these hot months. When you get there, it'll still be blazing hot. They have this crazy desert wind—the dreaded *Khamsin*—that announces itself as a sudden violent dust storm. Don't try to outrun it, or try to stumble through it. Just hobble your horses and hunker your men down until it's over. It may take a short time, *or not*— it depends.

"One more thing. An army is only as good as the *vitailles* it consumes. To that end, look for a good translator in Genoa or Venice, someone who can speak our language and Turkic or Arabic The translator will be a valuable asset when dealing with locals about available food and in getting reliable directions.

"A word about the leaders of the Saracens. Saladin is their inspired leader, their Sultan. He and his younger brother Nasr are vicious, and determined. They are committed to destroying us, killing every one of us. They are fanatical, horrible monsters — *fight furiously, never surrender*! Best to attack them head-on with blood in your eyes — rage will defeat them."

As his horse cantered forward, Lucan pulled himself out of his reveries. Then he looked about him.

Lucan remembered Rupert's words of advice. Upon seeing the wind-whipped cloud of sand approaching, he led his men to the shelter offered by the disintegrated *khirbeh*. He then ordered his battle group of a hundred mounted soldiers and support staff to hobble and secure their horses in a rough circle. Then they hunkered down among the ruined walls still standing as age-old sentinels against the ravages of time and weather.

Lucan wrapped his long scarf around his eyes, nose and mouth and lowered his head to meet his knees. His soldiers did likewise.

He moved his scabbarded sword more to one side to enable him to double up. He momentarily reflected on why his sword was on his right hip, whereas most Crusaders wore theirs on their left sides.

While he hunkered down against the storm, he thought back to when he was a mere snot-nosed lad. He fondly remembered Stefanus, his father's retainer, who persuaded his father to allow him to continue practicing sword-fighting using his left hand as a four-year-old. It was a rule that once little boys demonstrated a preference for their left hands, tradition required action.

His father had believed in his tribal tradition of lopping off all or part of the little finger of the left hand to make it much more difficult to hold a sword in that hand. Stefan had successfully argued against having Lucan's finger amputated, risking his position in doing so.

"Your Grace", Stefanus had said, hoping that his Lord Protector would see his point, "I believe little Lucan will have an advantage as a left-handed swordsman. Has My Liege seen how effective well-trained lefties are against righties? Lucan should be allowed to express himself the way he was born."

Lucan's father was adamant. "It's unlucky and also evil to be a lefty. So say the sages. '*Sinistra*'—left-handedness—is the work of the Devil."

"Your Grace, let me work with little Lucan, and he'll make you proud of his swordsmanship."

Lucan's father later would die on some unknown and arid field in the Holy Land, his blood spilled and thirstily absorbed among the weeds and the dry sod. He was totally committed to the righteousness of the cause. He believed in the Old Ways, devotion, duty and tradition over all else.

He believed with every fiber of his body that Jerusalem should be the capital of a Christian Kingdom, freed by blood and sacrifice from the heathen Saracens. And until Stefanus had convinced him otherwise, he had adhered to the strict doctrine of right-handedness.

Stefanus had won that war of words, and Lucan was grateful to the old man, his teacher, now deceased, for speaking up and thereby allowing him to keep his pinkie. As heir to his father's fiefdom in the Holy Roman Empire, he had had many duals with sword and sabre, and had proven himself to be a superior swordsman

Lucan loved Stefanus; he was the father-figure he conjured up in his mind, much more than his actual father, who was absent for long periods of his son's life. Recently, possibly out of a yearning for the old man, he had reflected upon the many discussions and salient advice he had received over the years. He had also been visited at night by Stefanus' ghost, especially during the hectic preparations for departure on the Crusade.

While Lucan was in Genoa, sleeping in an inn close by the port, Stefanus had come to him in a vivid dream. He advised Lucan to pull out of the Crusade, telling him that he should go back home, that the Crusade would be a disaster and that Death would try to take him; Death would be in a tussle for Lucan's life.

"Listen to me Lucan. I am your old friend and advisor. Do as I say if you heed good advice and want to return home alive."

Lucan was visibly shaken by the revelation. Stefanus' shocking advice was in direct contrast to that of his father's. But he had no time to contemplate their conflicting counsel. His men were expecting him to lead them to victory against the heathen Saracens. Even if he had wanted to, it was too late for him to back out.

On board one of the two sturdy ships which brought him and his soldiers to Acre, in the middle of the storm-tossed Mediterranean, Lucan pondered on the meaning of life, as the tiny ship swayed, creaked and dipped into a trough of darkened water, hesitated, trembled up to its masts and then bravely started to climb out the other side.

Wind-whipped frothing foam swelled all around the faltering, shuddering boat. He thought about the unfathomable depth of the sea beneath the waves, each drop of water bound to the other in an all-encompassing network of oneness, of cooperation and solidarity.

We must learn from the water, he thought. *Woven together and powerful, solid and almost inseparable.*

Lucan's thoughts came roaring back to the present. The desert storm was now upon them, swaying and buffeting horse and soldier alike. It roared through the scattered encampment, howling with an incessant urgency that Lucan thought must be similar to that at the entrance to the Gates of Hell itself. The wind whipped and propelled each tiny grain of sand into a stinging weapon, viciously searching for any exposed skin to strike. The horses whinnied and nickered loudly, constantly battling to keep their rumps up against the shrieking and wailing blasts.

After a violent storm-tossed night, the sandstorm gradually blew itself out. By sunup, the winds had subsided. Lucan quickly gave orders to Percival. Scouts were sent in four directions to search for water and food. After twenty minutes, two scouts on speedy steeds came back with good news. One had found a small stream with sparkling, clean water, and the other reported that there was a large flock of sheep and goats on a nearby hill.

Lucan sent his soldiers to the stream with their horses. He sent Percival, the translator and a small squad to bargain with the shepherds.

After a lavish meal of roasted lamb augmented by buckwheat, Lucan led his soldiers on. The weather after the storm was humid, with the rising sun across cloudless skies heating up the day. Lucan had been advised to travel in a south-easterly direction, which he did by following a rough path between the sunrise and the midday sun.

Lucan's mounted cohort clanked along, the sounds of metal hitting metal and the snorting of their horses a constant reminder that his was a warrior expedition into a desolate land, searching for the elusive enemy intent on destroying them in order to regain a much-contested city. Jerusalem was as much an aspiration as it was the ancient Holy City of David and Solomon the Wise.

The burning midday sun played tricks on his eyes; shielding them, looking through droplets of sweat from his brow, he could see nothing but vibrating haze in the far distance, where he had been told there were hills, marking the end of the coastal plain. The hills, once they reached them, marked the beginning of the climb toward their objective—Jerusalem.

The horses cantered across dried fields of baked earth; nothing but coarse weeds, clumps of desert grass and small cacti grew there. Occasionally they passed a stand of wizened, hardy elms, wild fig trees, palm trees and scattered groves of olive trees, a hint that at one time the coastal plain had been verdant and thriving.

Lucan kept looking through shielded eyes for signs of pending danger. He had been told that the Moslems under the leadership of Saladin were intent on reconquering the entire area, not just Jerusalem, but all the territory now under Crusader control.

At long last in the distance he saw what he had been expecting; a band of horsemen in front of the dust which their horses were throwing up. This was what he had come to the Holy Land to accomplish; to reinforce the Holy City, and to remove the Saracen scourge, once and for all.

He turned swiftly toward Percival. "Sound the alarm. Enemy horses are approaching."

Lucan reached a small grove of olive trees on a gentle downward slope. Up against one of the trees, he caught himself admiring the gnarled, twisted tree closest to him; he thought about how old the tree must be, and how hardy it must be to have survived all the myriad droughts and storms that had afflicted it. Peering through the thicket of its leaves, he kept his eyes on the oncoming horsemen. He could make out the turbans on their heads, the colors of their horses and in some cases the weapons they carried, despite the dust their horses were churning up.

He signaled Percival to approach. "Roughly fifty. Coming at us at a canter. I don't think they've seen us, probably because they're looking into the sun. Get the men ready; at my signal, we engage."

Lucan waited for another minute, waiting as the Saracens crested a slight rise across an open fallow field. He looked back, raised an arm and screamed "Charge! For Country, Christianity and God Almighty!"

Lucan's horsemen plunged, galloping headlong down the slope. The Saracens became aware of the danger through the bloodcurdling yells of the Crusaders. The leader of the Saracens took one look at the onrushing hoard and decided to turn and flee; his band of fighters followed, willy-nilly. The Crusaders were fast closing the distance between the opposing forces.

"Chase them! Onto them!" Lucan screamed, his spittle flying into the wind.

Lucan's steed closed the gap, and he saw the closest Saracen horseman right in front of him, frenziedly beating his horse on the thigh and loins for encouragement.

Lucan swung his body into a forward lunge, his left hand swinging his powerful sword down in a chopping motion. The turbaned Saracen let out a spine-chilling scream and started to topple off of his saddle.

He threw up his hands and a spear flew from his grasp, smacking sideways onto Lucan's left leg. Lucan chopped at him again. The Moslem slumped forward, his body falling between the horses.

By this time the rest of his mounted soldiers had caught up with the Saracens. The leader turned to face the Crusaders, nothing but hatred in his eyes. He and a small remnant of soldiers went into battle with blood-curdling shrieks, to no avail. They died a swift, valiant death.

Salah ad Din became the Sultan, the leader and founder of the Ayyubist dynasty upon the death of his father.

As a child he had many brothers and sisters. Most of his brothers died due to childhood illness. He was the eldest son, and Nasr ad Din, his younger brother, was the 'spare,' in case something untoward happened to him.

The two brothers grew up together, constantly fighting, constantly in competition with one another. Saladin (as he was later called by the infidel Crusaders) was almost always the victor. Nasr eventually contented himself to being his older brother's loyal lieutenant.

The Ayyubs were ethnic Kurds, who influenced other Moslem tribes around them. Gradually, through conquest, the divergent clans coalesced into one societal group—the Saracens—who consolidated and expanded their lands and their faith. At this crucial point, Europe's rulers began their efforts to establish a Christian kingdom in the Near East, with Jerusalem as its capital.

Saladin's fame grew as he defeated the Crusaders in key battles. He and his brother Nasr earned a reputation for extreme cruelty to prisoners who fell into their hands; the brothers looked upon those who surrendered as being 'inferior' fighters to those who sacrificed their lives for their cause. Always wary of overplaying his hand, Saladin preferred a veiled fist; he used guile to draw the Crusaders' superior forces into cleverly disguised traps where he would have the numerical advantage.

Nasr spent a great deal of time on strategy and on torture. He supplied his warrior brother with the tools to wage war and eliminate their enemies.

He had studied the Crusaders' methods of torture, and found them wanting. He reported back to his brother. "Our methods of torture and 'persuasion' are far better than the infidel's, o brother. And more humane: if a prisoner survives our '*Arba-ein*,' then we will even give him a chance to convert to the One True Faith before considering whether he's worthy of living."

Saladin smiled at his brother. "*So he converts and* then *we kill him*?"

Nasr chuckled at his brother's interpretation. "No, My Liege. If he converts with sincerity to our holy Moslem faith, his life will be spared. If he survives the '*Arba'ein*,' then we give him the chance to live the Correct Way as dictated by our Prophet Mohammed."

"And what is the likelihood of surviving the '*Arba'ein*?"

Nasr's dark eyes narrowed. "We have used the rounded stones on the sides of Wadis many, many times. The ones who throw the forty stones are either our brave soldiers or bereaved family members of our hallowed Shahids, who sacrificed all for the love for Islam. We have never had an infidel prisoner survive."

Lucan's forces were 'blooded'; they felt good about their victory. They continued onward until they reached the foothills of what their mapmakers had called 'the Jerusalem Hills.'

Lucan surveyed the surrounding hills and opted to make camp for the night on the crest of a hill. The accompanying cooks served the troops more lamb in a vegetable broth. As the sun finally set over the distant Mediterranean Sea, he posted guards, and promptly fell asleep, exhausted.

The next morning was hot and humid. Some of the soldiers were heard to complain about the arid conditions. Others complained about boils and blisters in sensitive areas of the body. Still others about the cursed swarming flies which constantly buzzed around their heads, always looking to alight on their faces, their eyes, their lips.

Lucan heard about some of his soldiers' gripes. He gave orders for some precious stored ale to be administered; the cooks prepared grain porridge and distributed flat bannock bread, which they still had in plentiful supply.

"I want them to be in good spirits for our ride toward Jerusalem," he muttered to Percival. "And be ready to take on any Saracens we encounter. They're as thick as thieves in this area."

"Aye, Milord. They'll appreciate the ale—and the porridge."

Lucan nodded. "And take them to the stream to soak up some water—the horses too. There's sparse grazing for them in these parts."

The burning sun was rising higher once the cohort broke camp. To Lucan the occasional clanking and rattling sounds coupled with the snorts of their horses as they rode eastward were happy sounds. Not one of his soldiers was hurting so much as to take away the anticipation of encounters with the enemy, or the joy of riding into Jerusalem, the capital of the Crusader Kingdom.

The hills grew higher as they advanced. Here and there Lucan could see signs of human activity. An olive grove, with some pickers among the trees, and blankets and baskets on the ground; terraced areas where the sparse rainfall had been carefully channeled to grow vegetables and wild corn; a collection of whitewashed hovels where some children played outside.

Lucan led the cohort up the slope of a hill into a small rising valley. He ordered a couple of scouts to go forward to check out the terrain ahead. There were more terraced slopes and higher hills ahead of them. He signaled Percival to ride with him. "If I were planning an attack, this would be the perfect terrain for it," Lucan said. "I hope our scouts report back soon. And once they return, I'll send out new ones."

"Milord, I'd send them out now. Otherwise, we won't have eyes and ears constantly ahead of us."

Lucan agreed; he didn't mind being corrected. Percival was an experienced campaigner; new scouts went out ahead of the cohort.

Lucan led his horsemen onto part of the old Roman road, built by slaves more than a thousand years earlier. He noticed that the Romans had used large amounts of basalt chips, flint flakes and tailings taken from small quarries close by to firm up the roadbed.

Lucan and Percival led the cohort through a narrow valley which was dotted with olive and elm trees. Flint and rock pilings were everywhere, some of them arranged in walls, others in mounds.

Percival looked around him nervously. "I—I don't like this terrain, Milord—"

Suddenly, they were attacked. Screaming hordes of white-turbaned Saracens pounced from their hiding places among the walled rock pilings. Lucan screamed. "Attack! Fight for your lives!"

The Crusaders had a numerical advantage initially, but they were so engrossed in repulsing the foot soldiers milling around their horses that they didn't comprehend the danger they were in until it was too late.

A force of screaming mounted horsemen blocked the exit to the narrow valley, and a similar force appeared from behind a hill to block the other end; the Crusaders' horses were hemmed in by the walled rock pilings.

Lucan fought desperately, aware that he had been fatally tricked by the wily Saracens. He saw Percival dragged off his horse by three Seljuk warriors, fighting all the way down to the black earth. Through the corner of his eye he observed Percival being speared, his mouth wide open, his astonished eyes not accepting what was happening to him.

The Saracens used a classic pincer attack, driving the Crusaders' horses and dismounted soldiers up against the insurmountable flint walls. Lucan was pierced through his armor on his right side, and in the fury of battle a screaming Saracen knocked Lucan's sword from his grasp. He reached for his spare, a shorter seax, which he had attached to his saddle, and fought on.

The narrow valley was strewn with dead and dying men and horses. The screams of men on both sides were indistinguishable. Still the battle raged on.

Lucan fought wildly, fiercely, like a man possessed.

Eventually a Saracen horseman was able to spring from his own horse and knock Lucan down. He hit his face hard against the flint pilings, drawing blood. His mouth felt metallic, his lips, tongue, cheek and forehead were badly gashed. Blood poured freely from his wounds.

Still he fought, wrestling a Saracen to the ground and robbing him of his barbed flail. He continued fighting, sending three additional Saracens to meet their Maker.

When he was finally stripped of his weapon, he dropped to the ground completely drained and exhausted, but was still able to breathlessly pant, *"you beasts. You beasts...."*

Lucan, bleeding from wounds on his torso and face, was hauled into the tent of the Saracen brigade commander, Murshid ibn Bakr ibn Ahmad, together with half a dozen Crusader survivors, most more dead than alive. Lucan's hands were bound tightly behind him.

"What do we do with the prisoners, my commander?"

The commander looked at the Crusaders on their knees or barely standing in front of him. He approached Lucan, who was forced to his knees by his guards. "Is this the one who caused the death of so many of our brave soldiers, all of them holy *Shahids*, all now in Heaven with merciful Allah?"

"Yes, my commander. He's the one."

The Saracen approached; Lucan's eyes reflected the hatred he felt for the Saracens.

"We have too many of their cursed knights who we are going to ransom, from the battle up north. We will make slaves of the all the others, but strip this one; dress him only in an *awrah*. Then take him to the *wadi* and thrust him down into it…."

"Yes, my commander."

"Also, summon some soldiers and any local relatives of our brave soldiers who have sacrificed their lives for the glory of *Allah*."

Lucan was forcefully removed from the tent. Rough hands stripped him of his armor and then his clothing. He screamed when they pulled his clothes from the wound on his side. They put a loincloth on him, then trussed him securely onto the back of a horse. The horse bounded forward; its movement under him felt like stab wounds on his side. He passed out.

When he regained consciousness, he came to slowly, painfully. He felt himself lifted bodily down something rough. He was sitting up against the side of a pit, something sharp pushing into his bare back. The sun was blinding. Flies were everywhere, in the corners of his eyes and on his lips. He shrugged his head violently, blinking, trying to focus.

Voices, he heard voices, guttural, yammering away.

He looked up into the unforgiving sun, screwing up his eyes to see where he was and what exactly was going on. He caught a glimpse of turbaned people standing looking down at him. He tried to speak, but his tongue felt like a bloated, lifeless piece of salty meat; his mouth was devoid of any spittle.

I hurt... pain all over.... I'm in a pit of some kind...I can't move my hands... tied behind my back.... Stefanus... yes, kind and thoughtful Stefanus...I should've listened... what happened to the unity and the solidarity of water... and Mathilde, dear, sweet Mathilde, so far away... is she real.... My side hurts so much... so does my face.... My father... my father's buried here somewhere... just bones... What happened to our scouts... didn't warn us... I should be somewhere else... what am I doing here....

He heard voices...*Arba'ein*... they're repeating...*Arba'ein*. What does that mean....

The first rock caught him by surprise. It smacked down hard right next to him, reverberating.

The next one hit him squarely on his right knee. He screamed in pain, tried to struggle to his feet… couldn't.

You beasts… you gescheisene beasts!

The next rock hit him on his shoulder, right on the bone. He screeched… *the pain… oh the pain….*

The following rock….

NOTES: "The Crusader" came to me as a story to write, since the theme of the month of my writers' group was "Ghosts, Monsters and Beasts." Due to my exposure to European and Near Eastern culture, including the topography, geography and the history of its diverse, polyglot peoples, I wrote the story quickly, filling in information I knew regarding the Crusaders as well as the Saracens.

One important aspect was concocted: Saladin didn't have a younger brother named 'Nasr.' If he *had*, I don't believe that the brother would have survived for very long. Siblings were eliminated by rulers in those days, because they feared a coup, a seizure of power on the part of a brother, or even a son.

"Uneasy lies the head that wears a crown."

12

True Love

*J*enny had a difficult childhood, riven with periods of sickness and troubling weakness, for which no doctor could find a remedy. Born into a large Polish-Jewish family, she had moved with her parents and siblings to Vienna, then the capital of the diverse and polyglot Austrian—Hungarian empire.

The move had not been an easy one. It had been brought about due to grinding poverty and famine in Austrian Poland. Jenny's father Moshe Chaim decided that it would be better for the family to settle in glittering Vienna, where he believed they would have an easier life.

Emperor Franz—Josef was a benevolent ruler, who encouraged equality among the diverse citizens of his far-flung empire. Vienna at that time rivaled Paris with its many cultural and scientific accomplishments.

When Jenny was eight, a doctor finally diagnosed her as having a problem with her thyroid gland. She was prescribed pills, which seemed to work for a while. Years went by. Her father had opened a small general store in District II, the Jewish area across the Danube Canal from the city proper. Jenny, like several of her brothers and sisters, helped out, sometimes serving customers, running errands, delivering purchases, running to the post office, and occasionally having to buy needed groceries at competitors' stores, in order to keep their own customers happy.

When she was thirteen, Jenny came down with a particularly severe thyroidal attack. She was confined to bed for weeks. Spanish Flu was raging in the city; it was fortunate that she and her family avoided the pandemic. In addition, food and firewood were very difficult to find in a disemboweled and ravaged Empire, the result of being on the losing side in the Great War.

That winter was particularly harsh; even potatoes and turnips were hard to find. Wooden fences were mysteriously plundered during the freezing winter nights, to afford a family a few hours of heat in their frozen homes.

In the spring, Moshe Chaim was so concerned about Jenny's condition that he paid for doctor visits to their little flat on *Kleine Pfarrgasse* in the Second District; the results weren't promising. A thyroid problem was diagnosed. A specialist advised them to travel to Frankfurt as soon as they could to see the renowned Professor Doktor Karl-Heinz Waldheim. This famous doctor boasted favorable results in areas of medical research which were still in their incipient stages of exploration. Medical science was still researching the roles of the various organs in the human body. The thyroid gland's function was still a mystery; its role in the metabolism, growth and development of the human body was still decades away.

Moshe Chaim gathered all of Jenny's available medical information, and sent it together with a cover letter to Doktor Waldheim in Frankfurt, Germany. In it he inquired as to the cost of a consultation with the renowned doctor. The reply came back two weeks later. Jenny's condition continued to worsen. With considerable difficulty, Moshe Chaim raised money for the consultation, as well as for the projected three-day journey by train, with a stay in a guest-house in Frankfurt, plus frugal meals along the way.

By the time father and daughter left on the trip, Jenny had lost a considerable amount of weight, and was always tired and lethargic. Dr. Waldheim gave her all the tests available at the time, and suggested surgery as the only realistic solution to her problem. The good doctor gave Moshe Chaim his estimated fee for the surgery, which amounted to twice Moshe Chaim's annual income. Moshe Chaim asked whether he could pay in installments.

But of course, the good doctor said. *I've never turned away patients due to their inability to pay in full. I would like to operate as soon as possible; when can you have the young lady back in my office in preparation for surgery?*

Moshe Chaim consulted with his rabbi before he decided to embark on the journey; Reb Yaacov was on very good terms with a rabbi from Frankfurt, who kindly offered to house the Viennese visitors after Jenny's operation. A month later, at the tender age of fourteen, Jenny underwent a partial thyroidal removal. It was a difficult operation; very few surgeons knew enough about the possible effects of such an operation at the time.

Jenny and her father returned to Vienna in due course. Jenny grew into womanhood with no further apparent complications. She gained weight, making certain with her mother's help to eat the right prescribed foods for her condition. She continued her schooling, and matriculated with her classmates in the district school.

Vienna had become the oversized but still very lively capital of a greatly-reduced country. The Jewish community reached the height of its cultural influence, adding to every artistic and cultural field. Great figures of the era included the writers Franz Werfel, Stefan Zweig, Arthur Schnitzler, Joseph Roth and Karl Kraus; the composers Gustav Mahler, Arnold Schonberg and Anton Webern; Sigmund Freud founded psychoanalysis, and many others contributed their talents for the common good.

Not all of the Jewish luminaries were men; there were a small number of women who achieved high social and cultural prominence on their own accord, but they were the notable exceptions. A few years later, Hedy Lamarr would achieve great fame and fortune, but only after she had fled Nazi Austria to become the queen of Hollywood and a brilliant inventor as well.

In Austria, there were very few fields open to women; Jenny was fortunate to be hired by a nearby religious school as a kindergarten assistant teacher. For the next several years, she gave of herself to other people's children, treating them as her own.

It was during the joyous traditional *Fasching* season, between Christmas and Lent, that Jenny went to one of the numerous Festive Balls with a close girlfriend. Depending on one's social class, many in Vienna's multi-ethnic population were drawn to attending at least one of them. All of the many high-spirited Balls were held in various palace reception halls, in Municipal anterooms or in in large assembly rooms or ballrooms open for a fee to the general public.

At this particular ball, amidst all the press of happy revelers, Jenny met a young cellist, getting ready to play his instrument accompanied by the ensemble of his orchestra. Above the heady cacophony of hundreds of eager voices, all intent on having their own heard above all the others, she exchanged a few sentences with the mustachioed young musician.

They agreed to meet after the festive Ball was over, in the early hours of the morning. Jenny realized that she had promised her parents that she would be home by midnight, but the lure and excitement of a meeting with this intriguing musician outweighed the certain admonition and censure almost guaranteed on the following morning.

As the convivial and high-spirited Ball wound down, the musicians played their last familiar lilting refrains. Attendees were crowding around the two cloakrooms to retrieve their winter coats and hats. Jenny and her friend waited patiently for the orchestra members to reappear.

Finally the young cellist approached, carrying his instrument in a canvas cover.

Jenny was able to have a meaningful conversation with him. He introduced himself as 'Siegfried,' and said that he lived with his parents in another part of town. Jenny said that she too lived with her parents and siblings in District Two. To which Siegfried confessed that he also lived with his brother, but that he and his family were very secular.

Without really saying the obvious, the young man and young woman attested to their availability, and that they were both of the Jewish faith, notwithstanding the wide gulf in their beliefs. A follow-up meeting was arranged, at Dremel's Coffee House, one of the finest coffee emporiums in all of Vienna.

Jenny accepted her parents' reprimands for her tardiness with patience and apologies. In due course, she met with Siegfried at the celebrated coffee house.

Jenny was surprised how easily the two of them settled into easy banter, almost a familiarity. Even though Jenny came from a very religious background, she was known in family circles as a rebel. Sometime in between her bouts of ill-health, she had shocked her stalwartly conservative parents by telling them the she wanted to become an actress; her parents felt that actresses were a slightly higher version of a lady of the evening. She also caused consternation by declaring that she wouldn't want to marry a '*fromm*' (deeply observant) person in an arranged marriage, and that she wanted to choose her betrothed by herself.

Siegfreid had astonished her by saying that he had been accustomed to attending synagogue just once a year, on Yom Kippur. His family didn't even light Shabbat candles! Jenny made a mental note to try to influence this deficiency if they were to get involved. She laughingly said that Siegfried was a 'Jewish *Goy*'; he wasn't unduly offended.

After the initial meetings, Jenny and Siegfried sought one another's company on a regular basis. She asked him about his career as a cellist. He mentioned that he was trying to enter the *Diplomatenschule* in order to become accredited as a diplomat. He explained that he wasn't able to make a decent living as a musician; he did well during the festive *Fasching* season, but didn't make much money during the rest of the year. Even though Vienna was the 'City of Music,' there were just too many musicians chasing too few engagements.

Siegfried explained about the prospective career change: Jews were generally barred from the civil service in Austria, but he hoped that his father's close relationship with a former commander of his from the Great War would help.

The former commander had risen to become the Deputy Foreign Minister in the Austrian Government. To Siegfried's delight, his father's war-time connection bore fruit. He was admitted to the diplomat's training school. With his natural gift for languages — he spoke seven — he found much of the course-work relatively easy.

Jenny swore a sister to secrecy, and told her that she was in a serious relationship with a cellist. Her parents sensed that something untoward was going on behind their backs, and pressed her for information, but she was reluctant to provide details. She instinctively knew that her parents would disapprove of her choice.

By the time Siegfried graduated, he and Jenny were exclusively seeing one another. Jenny told her parents and siblings that she was serious about a young man, and that he was Jewish. That allayed some of her parents' misgivings, but they continued to press her for details.

In her conversations with Siegfried, the topic of having children came up.

"I'd like us to have at least two children… What do you think?" Jenny asked Siegfried.

Siegfried was more circumspect. "I want us to be established somewhere safe… it's becoming increasingly unsettled here in Austria. When we're safe and secure, then we can consider having children."

Jenny had a disturbing re-occurrence of her thyroid condition. The specialist who examined her warned her that she would always be at risk for adverse effects and potential damaging outcomes to her health.

"It is not advisable for you to become pregnant. If you do, it could lead to serious consequences for you, as well as the life of your child."

Jenny tearfully relayed this terrible report to Siegfried.

He held her close.

"Don't worry, darling. By the time we decide to have children, they may find a cure for your thyroid condition."

Jenny was determined.

"Having a child together is an expression of true love between a couple. We love one another, Freddie (her pet name for him), so we should try for at least one 'true love' child. As you said, things may be better in the future."

After Siegfried had graduated, he and Jenny decided to become betrothed. According to tradition, this required their parents' involvement: this was to be a formal first meeting.

Siegfried's parents, as uninformed as Jenny's, decided to host a get-together in their little dining room. Moshe Chaim, upon hearing for the first time from Jenny who exactly Siegfried and his parents were, refused to go to the home of a family who didn't adhere to strict dietary (kosher) laws.

According to Jewish tradition, the betrothed future groom's parents were to invite the future bride's parents to their home. A compromise was reached. No food or beverages were to be served, which was extremely unusual.

It was a stiff, formal first-ever meeting between the respective parents. Siegfried's mother was so overwrought that she extended her hand to Moshe Chaim, who was dressed in a long black caftan, or coat. A tall man, he smoothly declined the extended female hand, putting his hands behind him.

"I must apologize, my dear madam," he stated solemnly, "but I cannot shake your hand. It is proscribed by Jewish law."

The meeting between the families got off on the wrong foot, and didn't go at all well.

Jenny's parents did their utmost to dissuade her from getting married to Siegfried, who they diplomatically described as a 'non-practicing Jew,' as close to a rebuttal as possible.

Jenny refused to be budged. *"We're going to get married, and that's that! And I'm going to keep a kosher home."* This last was a sop to her parents, although she genuinely meant it.

Nothing in life goes according to plan. That's obvious to those who live it.

Siegfried got a consular appointment; he was appointed as Second Consular Officer at the Austrian Consulate in Cape Town, Union of South Africa. He told Jenny that he would be leaving within the week. She was unhappy about the appointment, but Siegfried assured her that he would send for her as soon as he could.

Jenny was persistent. "How long before we see one another once again?"

"Don't worry, Jenny. Once I arrive, I'll start the process to bring you over. I'll be working on getting my parents and brother over as well. The South African government is divided about who to support, Hitler or the Allies.

"Germany has a lot of influence there, but I understand that most South Africans lean toward the English. And there's a large, active Jewish community in all the major cities, so you won't feel totally isolated. Once you get there, you can start the process of getting your parents to join us."

Jenny declared that her parents didn't want to leave Vienna under any circumstances. "They are bonded to the place, as anti-Semitic as Vienna is. I've asked them if they would want to move. My father told me that he has many graves to tend, and many friends besides."

About a month after Siegfried left for South Africa, Hitler started a campaign to destabilize the legitimate Austrian government. The Austrian Chancellor Schuschnigg was ridiculed and embarrassed by Hitler when he visited the Nazi dictator. Hitler told Schuschnigg to prepare for a Nazi take-over. The writing was on the wall; Austria's days as an independent State were numbered.

Nazi agitation increased in Austria, adding to Jenny's stress. Siegfried made inquiries about how to get Jenny out of Austria; his diplomatic friends informed him that he and Jenny had to be married in order for her to leave.

A hastily-arranged proxy marriage was arranged in Vienna as an exigency. Siegfried's older brother Franz, who was just short of finishing his medical Boards was called upon to stand in. The marriage was a civil one, attended by the two families involved.

Once she was officially married, Jenny set about obtaining the necessary documents to get an Austrian exit visa. Sometime in January of 1938, Jenny arrived in Cape Town.

Before leaving Vienna, she paid a last visit to her doctor, which was required of her in order to satisfy both emigration and immigration requirements. Her doctor again warned her not to get pregnant, or face dire consequences.

Siegfried was very happy to be reunited with his newly-created wife. They set up home in a bucolic area behind Table Mountain, not far from Cape Town University. Jenny found a part-time job helping a local chicken farmer pack his eggs for market. She saved the money she earned until she had a tidy sum, and shipped the money to her parents in Vienna, using a diplomatic courier who Siegfried knew from work at the consulate.

Jenny was happy in her new surroundings. She found Cape Town a strange and exotic place, a mixture of Europe and Africa, topped off by beautiful tropical and mountainous vistas. She missed her siblings and her parents, but she concentrated on providing Siegfried with a kosher home. That was the one concession Siegfried granted his wife.

Jenny experienced some of the same troubling symptoms she had in Vienna; she was monitored by her new doctor.

In mid-March of 1938, Siegfried lost his position in the Austrian Diplomatic Corps, the result of Germany absorbing Austria into the Nazi Third Reich, known as the *"Anschluss."*

Siegfried had brought along his cello, so he transited smoothly back to searching for 'gigs,' as he once had in Vienna. Jenny continued working examining and preparing eggs for market, and continued to send money to her parents in Vienna. She kept in touch with them once they fled to Belgium to avoid being shipped to the east for 'relocation,' as many Austrian Jews were. It's not clear quite how Siegfried and Jenny decided to go against her doctor's orders and get pregnant. *Was it accidental? Or was it a deliberate attempt to grapple with fate, to take on the awesome responsibility of giving birth in spite of all the flashing warning signs?*

"It's our love child, Freddie, our attempt to produce a good human being, a citizen of the future."

She told Siegfried that she would do everything in her power to give birth to a normal, healthy baby, even though the risks were considerable. She guided herself carefully through the first trimester, and then the second. She began to believe that all of the warnings were just that—mere warnings. Her doctor was amazed at her tenacity.

She had bad days and better days. Siegfried was frequently out on 'gigs.' She was happy that he was busy, and besides, they needed the money.

By early 1939, Jenny was into her ninth month. In the German *Reichstag*, Hitler stated that the outbreak of hostilities between Germany and the Allied Powers was inevitable, and that the conflict would mean the end of European Jewry.

On January 22nd of that year, in Groot Schuur Hospital, about two miles from where Jenny and Freddie lived, she gave birth to a baby boy. When Freddie came to her bedside after a difficult birth, Jenny whispered to him, *"This is 'true love,' because no matter what happens to me, we've created our son, a member of the next generation, someone who will carry forward our dreams and aspirations."*

Jenny died of thyroidal complications exactly seven months later. Her son, her true love son, was named Henry Michael. I am that son.

13

Two Juicy Red Apples
from a Very Long Way Away

My commanding officer called me into his office, suddenly, unexpectedly. I entered, anxious. He was seated at his small desk, papers and files strewn around. He gazed at me, brows wrinkled, dark eyes searching my countenance. *"Henry, I've got a mission for you… something out of the ordinary."*

This was the Israeli Army, where formalities of rank are frequently dispensed with, especially from top down. After all, I was a mere Sergeant, and he was a colonel.

I must have mumbled something; he continued.

"We have a convoy leaving for Mount Scopus, the day after tomorrow. Our task is to ensure that our boys arrive safely, as much as we possibly can…. I want you to be at the Mandelbaum Gate, the day after tomorrow, wearing civilian clothes. Clear?

"Yessir — how do I get —"

"*I'm giving you -*" he busied himself scrawling on a pad, signing his name with a flourish -"*here, take this. It's a pass until tomorrow evening. Go home to your kibbutz. Leave right away. Pick up a pair of jeans, a tee shirt, sandals — be back here by eighteen hundred tomorrow. Report to me personally. Clear?*

"*Yessir— but what exactly is my mission?*"

He leaned back in his chair, dangling on the two rear legs, deftly twirling his pen in his right hand. "*A command car will take you to Mandelbaum. You know it, right? It's where tourists and Israeli Arabs come and go between us and Jordan. Our boys will be dressed as policemen. They'll all be lined up at attention in the quadrangle, and the -*" he moved the corners of his mouth downward, indicating his contempt and distaste -"*the Legionnaire officers and the United Nations people will be inspecting our boys. So close to them they'll be able to count their nose-hairs. Clear so far?*"

"*Yessir*", I muttered, not intending to interrupt him any more than I had.

"*Beseder. The day after tomorrow, at oh seven hundred, you'll be taken by command car to Mandelbaum. Once there, the officer in charge...*" he rummaged through some papers at the end of his desk ..."*Captain Shapiro... will give you a rucksack. Inside the ruck-sack will be smoke grenades and regular grenades. I know that you've practiced with both of them. So inspect them carefully, because you may have to use them.*"

I looked at him, at the same time forming a mental image of the quadrangle.

He continued. *"Your mission, Henry, is to stick to the inside walls of the parade quadrangle while our boys are being inspected. Be nonchalant, as if you're waiting for a travel companion. Keep your eyes on the upper parapets opposite you. The Legionnaire sharpshooters will be up there. If they start firing, quickly pull out the smoke grenades and smoke the area up good.*

"Our boys in the parade quadrangle will need immediate cover. Feel free to throw everything you have at 'em! Use your discretion. And the hand grenades are there in case you need them. If you do, at that point all hell will have broken loose. Clear?"

"Yessir," I said emphatically. I envisioned the absolute mayhem the colonel was describing where everyone on the parade ground, including Legionnaire officers, United Nations commanders, our 'policemen' and *I* were in mortal danger.

"What about a pistol?" I asked. Defending myself became an imperative, in my mind's eye.

He smiled ruefully. *"I wanted you to have one, but High Command shot me down."*

Within the hour, I boarded an intercity bus to Haifa. The bus cruised through the terraced, verdant hills west of Jerusalem, slowing down for the frequent curves in the road. At one of the few treeless curves, I looked westward, across the undulating coastal valley that was Israel's heavily populated narrow waist. I got a clear view of the long, glistening horizon of the Mediterranean Sea at the far side of the valley; fertile fields, towns, groves, *kibbutzim* and cities opposite my gaze, so close I could almost touch them.

I was reminded of when, during an officers' course I had taken, my military instructor had stood in front of a large topographical map of the area.

"*Over here,*" he had said, pointing to Israel's furthest eastern border around the funnel which pointed toward Jerusalem, "*this is where Israel is most vulnerable. This narrow band*" — he moved his pointer between the border demarcation line and the sea — "*is just fifteen kilometers wide.*" He paused for effect.

I did a quick calculation. *That's about nine miles. That's nothing — it would take a fighter jet, even when flying at sea level with the drag of rockets on its wings, only two minutes to reach the Mediterranean Sea. Whoever devised those borders and expected Israel to be able to defend them must have been crazy! Or possibly it was done* because *the borders were indefensible....*

I gave a thought to my mission. Israel and Jordan lived side-by-side, but beyond that geographical proximity, we might as well have been from two separate planets. They fluctuated between ignoring us, to hating and despising us; we, on the other hand, tried to engage them positively, with very little to show for it.

Two mornings later, I presented myself to Captain Shapiro. I looked like a typical, carefree tourist; the only accessory I was missing to make my disguise complete was a camera. He looked me up and down, and said, *"Follow me."* He led me out of the Israeli customs and passport control shed to a padlocked building close by. There he gave me the backpack.

"Have you been told what you're going to be doing?"

"Absolutely," I said.

"Beseder — check the contents."

I did: I counted six white-sided smoke grenades and six conventional green hand grenades.

"You know how to use them, right?"

I assured him that I did.

"Just to remind you — the Jordanians will inspect our boys, then they'll check the buses. Our troops won't leave even a cigarette on the buses, because that'll slow the inspection down. Once our boys reboard, the trip to Scopus begins. You are to remain in ready position until the last U.N. jeep leaves this compound. Understood?"

I nodded. I moved slowly into the quadrangle, casting sharp eyes on the tall parapets. I could see Jordanian Legionnaires' red-*keffiyeh'd* head coverings through the firing holes on their side of the quadrangle. I placed one sandaled sole up against the wall; after a short while, I switched to the other. It was a hot day. As the sun climbed higher, I started to sweat. I switched the rucksack onto my other shoulder, leaving a sweaty band where the ruck-sack had been.

A red tourist bus pulled to a stop immediately outside the compound, unloading a gaggle of tourists, all crowding around the baggage storage holds. A tour guide appeared; together with the driver, he directed the disbursement of the luggage. Once all the tourists had their luggage, the tour guide led them toward the Israeli customs shed. After several minutes, members of the group began filtering past me, carrying their luggage. They made conversation as they passed me, and I surmised from their appearance that they were Americans. We exchanged nods of acceptance and acknowledgment which passers-by share.

Just then, with a grinding mechanical sound, a convoy entered the compound. First came a white-and-blue United Nations jeep, followed by two well-used white buses spewing exhaust smoke; another U.N. jeep brought up the rear. The convoy continued noisily onto the far side of the quadrangle and parked against the far wall.

A contingent of Israeli 'policemen' spilled out of the buses, peaked police caps on their heads or in hand. They all carried white kitbags, their names emblazoned on their sides. Uzi sub-machine guns were slung on their shoulders. The 'policemen' dropped their kitbags to one side. They formed into two neat rows, their officer in front.

I remembered what I had heard. The cease-fire agreement between Israel and Jordan allowed a contingency of 'policemen' to occupy defensive positions around the periphery of the mountain exclave. The Israeli hilltop 'island' housed the original campus of the once-busy Hebrew University and the stately Hadassah Hospital. They wandered around the spacious, weed-infested empty grounds; the buildings themselves were beginning to look shabby, rundown and outdated, pleading to be utilized and maintained as they once were, before Israel's War of Independence.

The 'policemen'—all Israeli Army soldiers—bided their time, looking longingly across the city at the not-so-distant buildings of Israeli Jerusalem, just across the divide. Eventually, after two weeks of isolation, another relief convoy would arrive, and they would return to Israel proper.

No sooner were the 'policemen' in their inspection rows, than from out of the Jordanian side of the quad stepped five very starched and crisply dressed Jordanian Legionnaires followed by five anxious avuncular U.N. officers.

The red-*keffiye'd* Legionnaires walked slowly through the ranks of the Israeli contingent, so close to their enemy that they could count the nose hairs and discern the eye color of every Israeli standing at attention in front of them, just as my colonel had said.

This must have been one of the most bizarre military inspections anywhere on earth. As their inspection drew to a close, two

Jordanian Legionnaires and two U.N. Officers went through the two buses, just to make certain that the Israelis weren't trying to sneak heavy equipment up to their lonely mountaintop.

I cast a watchful eye on the Legionnaire officers, with a measured glance up at the Jordanian sharpshooters on the parapets. So far, all was going smoothly. The Legionnaires conferred with their U.N. counterparts. They all looked in the direction of their adversaries, who despite the sweltering heat stood at attention.

Four tourists, two couples, stopped in front of me to observe what exactly was happening on the far side of the compound.

"*English?*" one of the tourists asked, cryptically; he was dressed in khaki pants topped by a garish Hawaiian shirt. For a split second I thought I'd give him a sarcastic reply, but I nodded.

"*What's going on over there? Who are those policemen, Jordanians?*"

No, I answered, they're Israeli policemen being inspected by the Jordanians and the U.N. before the policemen depart for Mount Scopus.

The man in the Hawaiian shirt was inquisitive. "*Okay, but what and where is Mount Sco-piss?*"

I pointed in the direction which the convoy would take once it left the safety of the quadrangle. "*Out there, past the Sheikh Jerrah neighborhood of Jordanian East Jerusalem, there's a hilltop 'island' controlled by Israel, but is completely surrounded by Jordanian territory.*"

A woman who must have been Hawaiian—shirt's wife inter-jected. "*So what 'xactly are those cops doing on that mountain?*"

"*They guard the university buildings and the hospital that are up there. The hilltop is Israeli-controlled, but according to the armistice agreement, no civilians are allowed up there.*"

The other couple who had stopped to listen to the conversa-tion joined in. "*For how long do they go to the mountain... Sco-piss?*" asked the woman.

"*Yeah, and isn't there a danger of clashing with the Jordanians while they're up there?*" her male companion inquired.

"*Good questions,*" I answered. "*They go up by bus every two weeks, and relieve the squad who was guarding the hilltop. Then those guards who were up there come back down to Israel proper in the same buses on their return leg. And yes, there have been clashes between Mount Scopus guards and Jordanian forces, in which our policemen have died. But the U.N. does the best it can to eliminate clashes like those.*"

The man in the Hawaiian shirt shook his head. "*Is it worth your while to defend a hilltop which is completely cut off from the rest of your country?*"

I nodded. "*Yes it is. That hilltop is a part of Israel, and one day we'll incorporate it as a part of our country once again. So that students will again be able to study there, and faculty will be able to teach. And Hadassah Hospital will again be able to provide medical care to anyone who needs it, and doctors, nurses and staff will be there to assist them.*"

One of the women asked me where I'd learned my English, saying that I must be an American to speak it so well, "and with an American accent."

I decided just to say that I'd spent time outside Israel, and had picked up my English along the way. That seemed to satisfy them; many American tourists insist that locals address them in English, but they aren't inquisitive or perceptive enough to flesh out exactly which English accent locals use in replying, nor ask where they had acquired it.

The tourists were now walking past me in a large bloc; their tour guide hustled the stragglers forward, then rushed to the head of the line, tourists' passports in hand.

The inspection over, our 'policemen' started boarding the buses in orderly fashion. The Legionnaire's finest stood by watching them, mixed feelings of resignation and unhappiness in their eyes. The worried U.N. officers scurried about ensuring that all was according to schedule. The buses noisily started up.

The Legionnaire officers started to leave the quadrangle. The Israeli second lieutenant policeman who had been in front of his men gave a smart salute, which the U.N. officers returned and the Jordanians ignored.

In their packed buses, with windows firmly shut and with tight grilles across all the windows, the Israelis inside sweated and worried. The bus drivers followed tight behind the leading U.N. jeep, one bus right behind the other.

The Jordanian pedestrians and residents in East Jerusalem—most of them displaced Palestinians—knew that the convoy contained Israelis; they unleashed their venom and hatred in the form of phlegm, garbage and sundry rocks as the convoy slowly creaked, bumped, swayed and maneuvered through the ancient, narrow alleyways of their section of the city.

Recently there had been a new development: pans of animal urine and camel-dung had been hurled toward the occupants of the two buses, causing them to tightly close all windows. It was stifling hot in those buses during the slow half-hour hegira to the safety of their little island.

Once the back of the last U.N. jeep disappeared into Jordanian Jerusalem, my mission there was over. I left the ominous quadrangle to relieve the stress I felt. Outside on the road were a number of Israeli taxis, always stationed there during daylight hours because most returnees and 'first time border crossers' needed transportation to the city-center. A balding cab-driver engaged me in conversation. *"Anywhere I can take you?"* he asked in English.

I replied in Hebrew. *"No thanks. I'm army—a soldier."*

"Army? *What are you doing here dressed like that?"*

"I was protecting the Mount Scopus convoy while they were being inspected."

"Ah," the cab-driver nodded, understanding. *"I know that behind the scenes, you guys keep watch, just in case."*

"I'm glad that everything went according to plan."

"*Those poor bastards up there*," he said, hooking a thumb in the direction of Mount Scopus. "*Do you think that we'll ever get it back?*"

"*Don't know* when, *but we'll get it back some day*", I said with conviction. "*It's only a matter of time.*"

"*The* only *way that's going to happen, is that we're going to have to fight them for it, and the Western Wall as well.*"

I puckered my lips and nodded in agreement, kicking the ground with the toe of my sneaker.

"*Hey,*" the cabbie said, "*did you have a chance to take part in the crowd scene when they were filming 'Exodus' downtown last week?*"

"*No—I was on border duty, but I did get to see Paul Newman and Joanne Woodward face to face.*"

"*You* did*? Wow—how did* that *happen?*"

"*That day I was assigned to take a squad of guards to the roof of the dining room at the kibbutz overlooking the Bethlehem road. You know it, right?*"

He nodded. "*Yeah, Ramat Rachel, high up on the bluff overlooking Bethlehem.*"

"*So I was on the roof with my binoculars. I heard a vehicle pull up down beneath me. I looked down and there were Paul Newman and his wife Joanne Woodward stepping out of a Government Tourist Office limo.*

"*He looked up at me, shielding his eyes from the sun and drawled a long* 'Shahlohm…. How are you doing?'

"I raised my hand in greeting and gave him a 'Shalom' back, and then the tourist guide took them to the edge of the barbed-wire border below us and showed them Bethlehem in the distance."

The conversation over, I wandered back to the Israeli customs and passport control shed at the entrance to the quadrangle.

The customs shed was nondescript, bare-basics, built of hardy wood which bore the damage of years of wear-and-tear without a decent paint or lacquer covering to protect it from the elements. It was capped by a simple tiled gable roof. It was brightly lit. At one end there was a small office, a men's and women's toilet, and a small storeroom. A couple of large wooden crates with heavy thick black address inscriptions and several outsized jute sacks were stacked against the storeroom wall awaiting the expected arrival of a traveler in transit. The rest of the shed was given over to the task of checking baggage and the travel documents of departing and returning residents and tourists.

Down the center of the shed a long, fairly low baggage inspection bench ran practically the whole length of the structure. On one side of the inspection bench were a couple of customs and immigration officers' desks; the other side of the bench was intended for the travelers passing through.

A German couple was being inspected when I entered. They had come from Jordanian Jerusalem, where they had spent the night at the Intercontinental Hotel. I heard the man telling the customs official about their stay; the agent politely listened as he opened and checked the couples' suitcases. Finally he reached down and stamped the couples' passports, making a small notation in them.

I remembered reading about the newly constructed Intercontinental Hotel, which was partially built on top of an ancient Jewish cemetery. The Jordanian government had desecrated the graves in order to construct the hotel and its access road; they did it because they could, with intent.

A family of returning Israeli Arabs entered the customs shed on their way back to their village. They had been visiting some relatives in Jordan, and they were bringing back their belongings and acquisitions—large bundles of clothing tied with cord, heavy jute sacks filled with rice, flour and produce, and large cans of olive oil.

The head of the family wore a checkered black-and-white *keffiyeh* with black head-bands on his head and a western grey jacket over his traditional clothing. Sweating profusely, he labored to put all of the items on the customs bench, while his stout black-robed wife put some smaller bundles down and busied herself with their children.

The German couple left the customs shed, and headed towards the same cab-driver I had spoken with.

I turned my attention to the Arab couple with their five children. The amount of baggage on the bench was prodigious.

The customs agent busied himself with some of the larger bundles in front of him. The Arab returnee stood by a larger bundle, making a fuss. A distraction, I thought.

I noticed that he had stealthily placed a bulky sack on the floor by his left leg, and was moving the sack along as his other possessions were being inspected on the bench. Intrigued, I watched him come toward me. He noticed that I was observing him; his eyes pleaded with me not to say anything. I remained silent.

Finally, the customs inspection over, he hastily gathered his belongings from the bench directly opposite where I stood. The jute sack at his feet got mixed in with his pile of other possessions. He spewed gratitude at me, mixing Hebrew with Arabic. He began picking up the heavier, blanketed bundles. I stopped him and pointed to the uninspected sack.

"I want to see what's inside," I said with authority. He must have thought that I was an inspector dressed in civilian clothing, so he deferred to my take-charge instructions. The customs officials opposite me were by now busy with other returnees and some tourists.

He proffered me the sack, and I looked inside and ran my fingers through the contents; nothing but pungent coffee beans.

Obviously, he had felt that he was over the limit and would be charged customs duty.

With a knowing look, he raised the palm of one hand at me and went back to his wife, looking into other sacks which lay around her. Finally he grunted, and came back to me sweating and smiling profusely. *"For you — thank you, thank you."*

I looked at his hands, and saw that in each were two huge red apples. He pushed them at me. I took them, not wanting to attract unnecessary attention. The Arab family departed, one large sack and bundle at a time. I placed the apples carefully into my bulging pants pockets.

I hadn't seen apples quite like those in a very long time. They were large, red, and probably very juicy. Israeli apples were invariably green and slightly astringent. I should know: I had picked them during harvest time on my kibbutz.

My assignment over, I turned in the grenade backpack to the officer in charge of the border transit post. I then hitched a ride to the area around the King David Hotel in an army vehicle, and walked back to my observation post right on the border.

The day was hot and muggy, but at least there was a breeze. Downstairs in the kitchen I washed the apples and used a knife to cut them into slices. Some of my men came by to watch what I was doing. They were pure *apple* apples, not the crumbly kind: they oozed juiciness and sweetness. I glanced at my watch; I still had time to snooze a little before my self-appointed shift up on the roof.

Where did you get them, one of my charges asked, after tasting his slice.

I didn't hesitate. "*From Jordan,*" I said with a smile.

We all thoroughly enjoyed the sumptuous tasty treat.

Fast forward one year: we were once again assigned to border duty in Jerusalem, after another hectic year of tank duty on Israel's various borders, enduring blazing hot days and limitless star-filled chilly nights, sometimes exchanging canon-fire with enemy forces, sometimes at the ready while our infantry went in on some reprisal action or other.

I chose to be in charge of the same observation post that I had the previous year. The border neighborhood hadn't changed much; there were several new houses on our side of the border, and I noticed a couple of semi-completed houses down the slope in Jordan. The nurses' training school just behind our position was still active; I made a mental note to go over later and see whether I could convince a nurse to go on a date with me.

Once again I put myself down for two-hour stints of border watch on the roof. I settled into the routine; my men appreciated my standing guard just like them.

On one of my watches on the roof, I saw an officer standing guard on the Jordanian border post opposite mine. On his head he wore a bright-red *keffiya* with black *agal*, which distinguished him as belonging to the British-trained Arab Legion.

I don't remember who spoke first, but we started a conversation. He told me his name—Mustafa. He said he was married and had a couple of children. After the initial cautious exchange, we warmed up to one another, and saw each other's humanity.

We agreed to meet again the next day, agreeing on a time. It was a simple procedure for both of us to put our own names down for the 2–4 pm (1400–1600 hours) watch.

The following afternoon, Mustafa and I broadened our surprising friendship. His English was rather formal, indicating quite a bit of schooling but not too much actual practice in conversation, which loosens the tongue and removes inhibitions.

I was pleasantly surprised by his familiarity with western literature, especially British and American. He told me that he had read *Robinson Crusoe* and *Treasure Island* while studying English when becoming a Legionnaire. He had a passing knowledge of certain books translated from the French (Voltaire and Victor Hugo), and from Russian, especially Dostoyevsky. A particular favorite of his was Ernest Hemingway; he mentioned *A Farewell to Arms* and *For Whom the Bell Tolls* specifically. We had a discussion about some of the battle descriptions of *Bells,* which he found fascinating.

We got pretty personal too. He wasn't inquisitive about where my excellent English came from; I mentioned that I had studied in England, which was true. But I didn't tell him that I was born in South Africa because I didn't want him to erroneously believe that the Israeli Army recruited 'mercenaries' from around the world.

I mentioned that Israel's President had given me a citation for valor in battle. He wanted to know on which front, which border; I told him that it had been on the Syrian front, and that seemed to satisfy him. He asked me whether I was a career officer, and I told him that I was serving my compulsory two-and-a-half years as a non-commissioned officer.

He asked me where I lived, and I explained that I lived on a *kibbutz*, a communal farm. He told me that he had read about these farms in an English magazine.

He wanted to know whether it was really as idyllic as described. I told him that the feeling of 'all for one, and one for all' was palpable on the kibbutz, but that there was a lot of hard work involved. I told him that recently I'd worked in the kibbutz's fish ponds, and that I'd experienced considerable satisfaction in gathering, selecting and shipping tankfuls of carp and whitefish to market from the kibbutz's large inland commercial fish ponds in the Galilee. He told me about his wife Aziza and his two children. He explained that he lived in a nearby town, very close to the Old City.

"It's called Silwan. We have built a small house there, and in my spare time I am adding a room. We were connected to the — how do you say — the ehh — electricity lines last year."

Mustafa told me that he planned to stay on with the Legionnaires because the pay was decent and he had good prospects for advancement; there were few other possibilities of employment. He asked me what I planned to do after the army, because I had told him that I had just a few months more to serve in the Israeli Army. I told him that I didn't know, that I wanted to finish my studies, which would require leaving the kibbutz for the city.

By the time our two-hour shift was over, we had gotten over each other's differences; culturally, religiously, and temporally we came from very dissimilar backgrounds. I guess we viewed each other as weird, exotic specimens, capable of being dangerous, and yet, we were solicitous toward one another.

We agreed to meet the following day, he on his roof and I on mine.

The next day, we broadened and deepened our friendship. We discussed the possibility of war between our nations; I told him that we wouldn't be the initiator of conflict, unless we were pushed to the wall by alliances between Arab armies.

That possibility intrigued him; he thought about what I had said. "*So we are safe to attack you if we in Jordan don't sign a war agreement with Egypt?*" Even from the distance between us, I could see he was pointedly asking me, tongue-in-cheek.

"*Yes—that's my opinion, but don't take that to your High Command, because if you do attack us, there will be terrible damage to Jerusalem, and we will defeat you—you can be sure of that.*"

"*How are you so sure?*"

"*Of our being able to defeat you? Because I* know *that we are much stronger than you. We would thoroughly defeat you, and chase your remaining forces across the Jordan River.*"

Mustafa backed down. One thing I found admirable about him was his candor. "*I believe you're right.*"

We talked more, about world events, about movies, about new literature. Then he surprised me even more.

"*When all this is over….*" He looked around him. "*I mean, when you will be able to cross the border… that separates us, I want you to come and visit us, at our home. I invite you. Aziza is a very good cook. She learned to cook from her mother, who lives with us. Then you'll have a chance to meet my two little girls. When you can… come.*"

I told him I'd love to come and visit. I hesitated for a moment, and then told him what we both knew in our hearts to be true.

"*It's not going to be easy… to do away with this border which separates us. There would have to be a war, and a cease-fire, maybe an armistice. A lot of people on both sides will die. Then all the barbed wire and the land mines would be removed, and the city of Jerusalem would be reunited...."*

"So all this would be yours." Mustafa looked around him, posing his words as a statement, not a question. He mulled over them, slowly digesting them, as uncomfortable as they were to him. *"What would you do with us, after you have defeated us?"*

My answer was spontaneous. *"We would treat you humanely. We wouldn't chase you over the nearest border."*

"So you feel that you are more human than we are, because we threaten to throw you into the sea... the Mediterranean?"

"Extremism is never a good idea—I feel that all of us deserve to have a homeland of our own." He was silent for a long while, lonely in his thoughts, standing on the edge of his roof, his weapon slung across his shoulder.

Then he looked up. *"Henry, I would like to ask a favor of you. It's something unusual."* He had addressed me by my name for the first time. That for him was a big concession, as conservative as he was.

Mustafa told me he was a smoker, and that he craved a pack of Israeli cigarettes. *"Not only for the reason you suspect—I have another."*

I told him he'd be very disappointed; regular Israeli cigarettes were on the whole pretty ordinary. (*I'd taken up smoking for a while on my kibbutz, and I knew what I was talking about.*) He smiled, saying the other reason was that he'd love to show an Israeli pack to his men in his emplacement, and take it to his wife. I understood him. Although our two countries were neighbors, having something from Israel would be the equivalent of his having authentic moon rocks in his possession, from the *far* side of the moon, no less!

I encountered a similar jarring, eyes-agape-in-astonishment experience ten years later. I was then a graduate student at Cornell. Our professor invited our class of six graduate students to accompany him to Toronto, Ontario, to check on the progress of an innovative Japanese hotel being constructed.

Our class had been involved in the preliminary research, feasibility study and projected profitability for the Japanese construction company. While in Toronto, we had gone for dinner in an up-scale Oriental restaurant. Our professor was a close friend of the General Manager. The restaurant was built into the side of a cliff; the upper floor was at street level, and contained the dining area. Underneath were the kitchens, and underneath them were the storerooms. The GM took us on the 'Grand Tour,' as he termed it. We toured the dining room, then the kitchens, and finally the storage area at the base of the restaurant.

I recall the scene very well. There was a linen chute there which waiters two floors above utilized to clean up vacated tables by bodily lifting the tablecloths, which contained silverware, ashtrays, napkins and the like, and tossing them down the chute.

There, on the floor, surrounded by piles of silverware, ashtrays and a mountain of linen and garbage was a wizened old Chinese man — probably an undocumented immigrant — who slept there while performing the tasks assigned him.

Right next to the growing piles were the chicken-wired storerooms, brimming with large Number 10 commercial-sized cans of food of every variety, plus sacks of spices, herbs and rice. On each can and sack, I incredulously read "Made in the Peoples' Republic of China." We had never seen Chinese products in the U.S.; they were a source of amazement and wonder for us, as if they came from another planet.)

"Are you serious? Are you thinking what I'm thinking?" I asked Mustafa.

"If you mean throwing the pack of cigarettes over to me, yes — that's what I'm thinking."

I considered the wisdom of doing this, in contravention of military protocol and rules. *"We could both be in real trouble if we get caught — I mean very serious trouble."*

"Correct — if we get caught," he emphasized. *"But we could get out with it."*

"Get away with it," I corrected him.

"Right. And what would you like me to send over to you in exchange?" He spoke as if the transaction was a foregone conclusion, that the likelihood of getting caught was so remote it wasn't even a factor in our decision.

A carefree, swashbuckling little Devil suddenly appeared, sitting next to my left ear; he had swiped away the careful, cautious Angel who had formerly been sitting there, sending it flitting and spinning to the ground. *'Do it—do something bold!'* The hell *with it*, I reasoned, repeating the voice I heard in my ear. *Let's do something bold.*

I recalled the juicy red apples from a year ago; the temptation was too much to ignore. *"I'd like a couple of the biggest, juiciest red apples you can find."*

"Apples?" he asked, wanting to confirm my unusual choice.

"Right—two of your biggest, juiciest red apples," I repeated.

We each stood on the edge of our respective roofs, measuring the distance between our two emplacements, agreeing that an aerial transfer would be quite easy to accomplish. We agreed to meet the following afternoon to complete the transaction.

The next day we stood guard on our respective emplacement roofs. I had purchased a pack of green-wrapped Israeli cigarettes, and had a paper bag as well. I showed him the cigarettes, and just to ensure safe delivery, I showed him a rock which I had picked up on the roof. I placed both items in the paper bag, and tossed it over the border which separated us. It landed on the roof. He opened the bag, and gleefully showed me the pack of cigarettes.

Then he showed me the two apples, and tossed them to me in a balled-up newspaper. I caught them on the fly. When my shift was over, I took them downstairs. Some of my men stood around and inspected them.

"Where did you get them?" one asked me.

I smiled. "*By air — from Jordan.*"

❧

Mustafa and I had agreed to meet the following day at the usual time, but he wasn't there.

I saw Mustafa again the next day. He explained that he was called away on something to do with one of his little girls, who had had an accident on the way to school; everything was fine now, he said. He also related how incredulous his men had been when he showed them the pack of Israeli cigarettes, with lettering in Hebrew, Arabic and English.

"*I agree with you about the quality,*" he said. "*Is this the best you have?*"

"*No, they're very average. At my kibbutz, I used to get a pack or two of those* exact *cigarettes weekly, when I smoked.*"

"*Not much better than food for camels.*"

I laughed. "*Like hay — I agree.*"

"*But the effect was…* amazing! *We have never seen anything from your country. We think of you and your people as a nightmare visited on us to punish us for looking away from the Holy Quran. And when I told them how I got the cigarettes, they didn't believe me…. How were the apples?*"

"Delicious—loved them! I shared them with my men. Much better than the cigarettes, I'm sure."

We both laughed. I saw Mustafa three or four more times after that. If one day he didn't show up, the next day he would be there on his roof, explaining what had occurred to prevent him from being opposite me on the previous day.

The last time we stood facing each other, he once again reminded me—when eventually I would be able to cross that impossibly impregnable, taunting border—to come and visit him in his town, Silwan.

Jerusalem, the eternal, smiled her godly smile across the eons, oblivious of the passing of centuries; the distance in time and space separating Mustafa from me literally was a mile-deep canyon gauged erratically across the face of the earth, juxtaposing a modern creation with an ancient past to a recent contrived invention still connected to the Dark Ages.

My tour of duty on the border was coming to an end. Soon my tank brigade would be back on 'Red Alert' somewhere on Israel's borders. The threats to our tiny embattled State were many.

Mustafa and I had never shaken hands, had never broken bread, had never sat down over a cup of coffee, and yet, I felt that he had become a new friend; we understood each other. More importantly, we saw eye-to-eye regarding some important material and philosophical matters, the absence of which would have prevented our friendship from developing. Mustafa and I shared a commonality that I didn't have with many Israelis of my acquaintance.

After he and I finished our shifts that last afternoon, I never saw him again.

⟡

Almost exactly six years later, The Six-Day War in all its explosive ferocity was winding down; my brigade was involved in one of the largest tank battles in military history in the Sinai.

I first heard the incredible news that the Old City of Jerusalem was ours, that the Western Wall was in Israeli hands, when I jumped off of my tank 'somewhere in the Sinai.'

We had spent a day and a night penetrating the Russian-conceived Egyptian layers of static defense. Massive frontal cannon fire and paratroop involvement shook and finally toppled the vaunted 'Valley of Death' defenses, as we overcame the bulk of Egypt's armored resistance. Out in the open, our tanks continued to 'bag' enemy tanks in direct warfare; the Israel Air Force was active in zeroing in on the remaining Egyptian strong points, pummeling and bombarding to harass, harry and finally destroy them.

As I was sending my crew to get breakfast from a field kitchen on the morning of the third day of war, the news reached us of our astounding success in Jerusalem.

I'm not in the least religious, but my eyes brimmed with tears to the news that for the first time in two thousand years we had regained possession of the last vestige of Solomon's Temple.

We were not only tilling soil which our ancestors of old had tilled, we not only walked on the ancient cobblestones on which our forebears had trod, but now we could once again worship where our forefathers had worshipped two millennia ago, as free men in our own country. A country for which we had struggled and died, long ago and again, tragically, within our lifetimes.

The previous day we had broken through the backbone of Egypt's armored divisions, and what remained of their tanks and armored personnel carriers were in full flight; they were frantically trying to reach two mountain passes just to the east of the Suez Canal, and were easy targets for our tanks and fighter jets.

The reunification of the city of Jerusalem was a joyous celebration to all of Israel, after the stress and tension leading up to the war and the beginning of the conflict, when things still hung in the balance. The whole country went on an ecstatic, exuberant binge, relieved and thoroughly delighted about the seemingly incomprehensible, that its little army and air force had achieved such remarkable successes.

My brigade had been among the very first onto the Egyptian border to meet the threat of Egypt's moving into the demilitarized Sinai Peninsula with two armored divisions plus support forces. We were also among the last to be sent home, more than two weeks after the cease-fire. I got home to my then-wife and seven-month-young daughter and did nothing but sleep for almost forty-eight hours.

A couple of my army buddies came by to share their war experiences, and after a meal prepared by my then-wife, the topic of Jerusalem came up.

"*Have you been yet?*" Uri asked me. He had served on the Syrian front and had been home for more than a week.

"*Where?*" I asked, knowing that my blurted answer was, to say the least, obtuse. "*To the Western Wall, of course, you dumb-ox.*" Good-natured zingers were as customary in Israel as the speaking of Hebrew as the national language.

"*No, but I'd love to go. From what I've heard, everyone wants to go and touch it.*"

Nissim, my second buddy blurted excitedly. "*And* pray *there, to give thanks for surviving, for each of us, and for the nation.*"

I agreed with him. "*And give thanks for surviving.*"

Nissim continued. "*The Western Wall is like a two-thousand-year-old magnet beckoning to us, pulling us in. We can't resist. Now for the first time in a couple of millennia, we have our holiest site back in our hands.*"

"*Okay: let's go to Jerusalem* — tomorrow." I was excited by the prospect. "*And there's something else I want to do there, as well as seeing the wall. Nissim, you speak* Arabic, *don't you?*" I knew that Nissim's parents had come from Iraq.

"*Yeah, but why is that so important?*" he asked.

"*There's someone I want to look up there, across the old border, in a town right across from Jerusalem.*"

"A *Jordanian? Ata meshugah?* Are you crazy?" Nissim looked at me bug-eyed, searching for an explanation.

I told them the full story, explaining that Mustafa was a good man, even though he was on the opposing side. "*And his English is pretty darn good,*" I said, winding down the story.

"*So what do you need my Arabic for?*" asked Nissim.

"*Because we're going to have to ask for directions, you dumb-ox!*" It was my turn to be sarcastic.

The following day, just for variation, we decided to take the train to Jerusalem. We knew that the roads were chock-a-block with sight-seers, tourists and the curious. Though the train was full, we were able to get seats.

As the train wound its way toward Jerusalem, the railroad tracks incredibly were just tens of yards away from the former border with Jordan. We could see one-time Jordanian villagers peering at the train, and we stared back. We were two neighbors separated by mere yards, but the distance was unfathomable.

In between us there had been an international demarcation line; something that told them 'those olive trees are ours, those fields also. But over there — *that* hill, *that* little hammock of trees, *those* railroad tracks, that's *theirs*.

'All that was taken away from us and given to those interlopers. Those places are stolen from us, but if we bide our time, we'll get them back—we'll chase these Zionist infidels into the sea.'

Our separate religions, our divergent cultures, our distinct traditions, our diverse histories, our different ways of life, our very being — all ensured vehement animosity and resentment.

Our train arrived with a screech and a long hiss and thrum in Jerusalem railroad station. I took Nissim and Uri toward Abu Tor, an area I knew well; that was where my old border emplacement was. We had agreed to go see Mustafa first, before going to the Western Wall.

Walking through the familiar neighborhood, with rocky, sandy lanes between those one-and-two-story homes and bony pine trees was a thrill.

I felt as if I had been on border duty here in Jerusalem just yesterday. I had the feeling that I was *floating* forward, levitating a few inches above the uneven terrain.

My old emplacement came into view; it was now occupied by a large family who looked as though they had been residing there for years.

I looked back, over my right shoulder; there, through the copse of fir trees, was the nurses' training school, still in operation. The lilting, evocative song *'Jerusalem of Gold'* wafted across to me in the breeze; before the war, it had unofficially become Israel's second national anthem.

A few yards further on, past my old emplacement, there was no longer any barbed wire!

Even though I had been away fighting a war, this result of the war—as welcome and anticipated as it was—was surreal; the barbed wire had disappeared.

Every last vestige of the old inviolable border had been cleared away. And this had gone on all over the city, and beyond. Barriers were being torn down; whole anti-sniper walls were being broken up with jackhammers.

Again, I felt as if I was floating as we walked down the hill into formerly Jordanian territory. Right away, I passed by the Jordanian emplacement that had been opposite mine. *I must be dreaming*; all of this was so marvelous and astonishing that it couldn't really be happening.

The three of us went down into a little valley. Israeli 'command cars' were everywhere, with the drivers, beside them an officer or an NCO, and usually two or three soldiers zipping through the narrow, mostly deserted streets. We found an enterprising cabbie, who asked us in broken English where we wanted to go.

With a little prompting from me, Nissim explained that we wanted to get to Silwan, close to the Old City. After a combination of grunts, tongue clicks and rapid-fire Arabic, the cabbie opened his back door. He wanted to know which currency we had, using finger gestures. I whipped out some Israeli *Lira*, and he grunted in agreement.

Being the pragmatic cab driver he was, he realized that Israel was the victor in the recent war, and Israeli currency would be completely acceptable until the next regime change, if that ever happened.

Nissim explained that we didn't exactly know where Mustafa lived. "The cabbie will find the house for us."

The cabbie did just that, with a voice that sounded alternatively pleading, then cajoling, then beseeching, then humble. He finally stopped at the entrance to a dusty path which looked as if it was suspended in air, because it came to an abrupt end at the edge of a ravine.

We paid him, and the three of us walked to the end of the trail. There, constructed above some caves lying below, was a single-story cinder-block house, most of it painted blue; a small tattered Jordanian flag was mounted next to the entrance.

"The blue is to ward off evil spirits," Uri muttered. "The Arabs believe that evil spirits despise the color blue."

The house was small, but looked like the house I imagined it would be, with Mustafa painstakingly building it block by block. A well-tended flower-and-vegetable garden lay on either side of the heavy front door. I knocked; the heavy wood didn't produce much of a sound. An elderly woman, dressed in black with a head shawl answered.

I nudged Nissim, who launched into a long explanation of who we were. He frequently looked in my direction. After some comments from the woman, Nissim said, "This is Mustafa's home all right, but he is no longer here—he died during the war."

"What—*dead*?" Even though I knew all about the absolute tenuousness of life, Mustafa's death shocked me, shook me. "How? Where? When?"

Another long conversation in Arabic. "He died fighting on the ramparts of the Old City Wall, during the paratrooper assault." I recalled reading and hearing about the bitter fighting on and around Ammunition Hill, when our paratroopers cleared the way into the Old City, suffering heavy losses themselves.

Nissim continued. "This woman is your friend Mustafa's mother-in-law. She says that his wife is at the market with their children, and she's expected soon."

We were invited in. The room had large low-slung pillows arranged in a circle; we sat down and were served Turkish coffee out of a large, ornate *finjan*. On a chipped plate there were some cookies. Nissim popped one into his mouth. "*Ghorayeba*," he said. "Butter cookies—try one: they're delicious."

A short while later, a slender woman, also dressed in black, entered the house. She carried a wrapped, swathed baby in her arms, with a little girl following her as closely as a duckling follows its mother. We all arose. Nissim once again introduced us, looking at me as he spoke. The woman nodded, giving her baby to her mother and putting her string shopping bags down.

"I remember about you," she said to me in Arabic.

Through Nissim, I told her about my conversations with Mustafa, telling her that he had invited me home 'when it would be possible.' I told her that I considered him a friend, even though we were on opposing sides. I told her how saddened I was to learn of his untimely death.

She looked me in the eye. "Mustafa showed me the pack of cigarettes that you threw to him. And he told me about the conversations you had across the border. He told me that he liked you, even though you were a *Yahood*, a Jew, an enemy."

I again expressed my condolences, telling her that his death was a tragic consequence of war, and that in his memory and the memory of others on both sides who had perished, it was important to strive for peace between our nations.

She nodded, then she and her mother busied themselves in their little kitchen, and came out with plates of stuffed grape leaves, hummus, tehina and pita bread; these they placed on a low table between us. The little girl, with large expressive eyes, curious but cautious, clung to her mother's *abaya*. We ate. "Where is your other daughter? Mustafa told me at the time that you had two little girls." I asked—Nissim translated.

"Out playing with friends." She teared up, and looked down lovingly at her baby, lying so quietly in her arms, his eyes wide open. "And now I have Abdul: Mustafa was so proud of little Abdul." She got up and went over to a small credenza, bringing back a framed picture of her family. I recognized Mustafa, smiling broadly between his wife and children.

We talked a little more, sipping our coffee and nibbling on the food.

"We must be on our way," I said. "We have other things we have to do in Jerusalem. We come from near Tel Aviv."

She nodded, and got up, disappearing into another room. She came back and handed me a picture. I looked at it and saw that it was of Mustafa, in his formal Arab Legionnaire tunic, red *keffiya* and black headbands. He was smiling and squinting into the sun. "For you to remember him," she said.

We stood near the door, ready to leave. I felt awkward: this wasn't the way it should have been. I reached into my pocket and pulled out a wad of Israeli *Lira*. "This is for your children, for you to buy them something, from me—their father's friend, from a long way away."

She looked at the money before accepting it. She raised a hand, disappearing into her kitchen. She came back, pressing something into my hands.

I looked down and saw two bright red apples. She smiled, and spoke haltingly, in English. "For *you*—two red apples… from a very long way away."

14

Zeitgeist — A Memory

*T*he three famous writers had grown close during their idyllic sojourn in a rented villa on the French Riviera. At first, just Franz Werfel and Lion Feuchtwanger used to meet, getting to know one another.

Once Austria almost willingly rolled over and was incorporated into *Nazi* Germany, they were joined by Alfred Polgar. Werfel and Polgar had already been friends from their years in Vienna. Lion Feuchtwanger had been based in Berlin until the *Nazis* took over. Polgar was noticeably jittery when he first arrived at the villa; Werfel noticed that his old friend was agitated and edgy; he nervously chewed his fingernails and had a facial tic.

"Alfred ," intoned Werfel , "*relax….* You're among friends — we're safe here."

Lion Fuechtwanger concurred in breathless staccato speed. "*Exactly!* I think that Hitler will now be met with more… *courage* on the part of the western nations. They wrote off Austria because Austria was already so softened up… that it fell gratefully into Hitler's lap. From now on, Hitler won't get a free ride. Therefore, by that reasoning, we're safe."

"*Safe*, you say? I feel like *Houdini*, but I'm running out of escape techniques. Or maybe I'm more like an *alley cat* who's already cheated death eight times…."

Franz Werfel nodded. "Eight times means that you have one more in you…. I can identify with that. After my recent heart attack, I realize that I received a wake-up call from The Man Upstairs. That's why we moved here from Paris."

When Werfel suffered the heart attack, Werfel's wife Alma had taken a far more active role in his continued well-being than before. Through friends in the exile community, she learned of the artists' colony in the south of France, and had made arrangements for the two of them to spend time there.

There were other well-known playwrights, poets, writers, and men of the artistic world staying at the converted quaintly-shaped conical stone tower villa in the tranquil, craggy little town looking down on the azure Mediterranean, almost all of them former citizens of Germany, Austria or Czechoslovakia.

The little town itself was a home-away-from-home for many literati, artists and other cultural trendsetters attracted by its restful, easygoing ambiance. During the winter months, their numbers swelled; wherever possible, they came to bask in the mild climate, leaving the miserable cold of central Europe behind.

The town was serene and quiet, its houses lying lazily among the crags and rocks of the hillside, settling among the many trees which added to its rustic and carefree ambience. It was an inviting place where the sojourners could unwind between their forays into the distant nether world of literature, meetings with publishers, exploratory trips and book tours.

Now, however, there was a feeling of unease, a disquieting apprehension that a distant turbulence was approaching, something lurking which would damage their secure feeling that their isolation would protect them from any threatening storm.

The three writers frequently met on the patio or the sitting room of the villa, sometimes accompanied by Werfel's wife Alma, or Wertheimer's spouse Martha.

Franz Werfel, a short, pudgy man was never far from a cigar, even though his wife Alma had effectively banned what she termed "those disgustingly smelly, soggy sticks" due to his health condition.

Werfel was a long-time pacifist who in his novels explored themes of common humanity and idealized brotherly love. He had achieved world-wide acclaim in the early thirties with his historic novel *Forty Days of Musa Dagh*, about the brutal Turkish persecution of their Armenian minority during the Great War.

When Werfel had married Alma in 1929, they had embarked on a honeymoon trip to the Middle East. While in Damascus, they encountered some desperately poor urchins living in squalid hovels with their impoverished parents.

Upon further inquiry, Werfel discovered that they were members of the Armenian community who had survived a series of ruthless massacres and forced deportations some fourteen years before.

Werfel identified with the Armenians, drawing similarities to the treatment of Jews in certain reactionary, repressive countries in Europe.

Alma Werfel—or, as she liked to call herself, Alma *Mahler Gropius Werfel*—was a remarkable woman in her own right. A vivacious pretty woman who had aged gracefully, she had been married first to a world-famous composer and conductor, then to a world-renowned architect, and finally to Franz Werfel.

In between—and sometimes concurrently while her second husband was away on military service—she had been the consort to some of Europe's brightest luminaries. Her 'salon coffee chats' had been all the rage back in Vienna; it was possible on occasion to chat with the Chancellor himself, or at least a Cabinet Minister, and have a famous painter or an in-the-news celebrity from the theatre sit at your table and share insights with you.

An invitation to attend from the spirited hostess meant that one had 'arrived.'

Lion Feuchtwanger was a wiry, intense man thoroughly devoted to his chosen profession; he was a prolific writer of historical novels, plays and poetry. He and his wife Martha traveled extensively. He was a pacifist with egalitarian leanings, traveling to the Soviet Union in the late thirties, during which time he interviewed Josef Stalin.

He earned the ire and hatred of the *Nazis* by writing several best-selling books critical of racism and anti-Semitism, at the same time lampooning Hitler and fascism. (One of them, *Success*, is rated among the finest novels of the twentieth-century.)

Lion and his wife Martha had been on a book-and-speaking tour in the U.S. when the Nazis came to power in January 1933; they were warned by the anti-Nazi German Ambassador not to return to Germany.

"If you go back to Germany, Herr Feuchtwanger, we will never know what became of you. The Nazis will simply make you vanish. Poof!"

They had quickly relocated to France, leaving their ransacked and vandalized home in the hands of the Nazis.

Alfred Polgar was the oldest of the three friends. A first-rate raconteur, reviewer and essayist, he became a master of cutting humor and nimbly rolling prose in the cafes of Vienna. His earlier success had moved him to Berlin; he had enjoyed a huge following in the German-reading world. Once Germany embraced Nazism, he fled back to Austria, just ahead of the SS. He did the same thing in March of 1938, this time headed for Switzerland.

Eventually he moved to France, where once again he was confronted by the Nazi 'Brown Scourge.' (Much later, once safely in the U.S. after a harrowing and exhausting climb over the Pyrenees Mountains in transit to Portugal, Hollywood–based singer-actress Marlene Dietrich had wanted him to write her memoirs; nothing ever came of that potential artistic liaison.)

The airwaves and newspapers in Europe in the late 'thirties were filled with ominous and threatening news. When Czechoslovakia was mercilessly diced up and sacrificed to the Nazis by Paris and London, the three friends nervously took stock.

"Those *gutless* French morons, and those self-serving English *cowards!*" spat Franz Werfel, his anger overflowing. "They backed down in spite of mutual defense treaties. Who can you trust to stand up to the Nazis? Hitler is coming across as a damned *demi-god* to the German *volk* — he can do no wrong. Perfidious sons of bitches!" He chomped hard on his cigar, puffing furiously. He broke into a spasm of throaty coughs, his eyes bulging.

"Things aren't looking good… *not at all*." Alfred Polgar kept wringing his hands in animated anxiety. "Every day the Nazis grow bolder and brasher, and the western nations continue to give in and step further and further back. Someone had better remind them to grow some spine, and *quickly*."

Lion Feuchtwanger harbored a strong liking for the French; even though he had personally experienced incidents of blatant anti-Semitism while in Paris. He appreciated the freedoms that France espoused.

"You can't entirely blame the French: it was *Chamberlain* who met with Hitler and was convinced by Hitler that Nazi Germany's claim to the Czech Sudetenland was *legitimate*.... Hitler used him like a towel to clean his dirty hands with. Things are going downhill fast, like an avalanche gathering speed, obliterating everything in front of it. I don't know where all this is going to end," he muttered.

Werfel quickly responded to the hanging query. "*I know where —* The Nazis are going to grab everything that they want until the French and English finally stand up and say '*no more.*' And they have to do it from a position of strength. *Hah*! Is that too much to ask? Hopefully that'll be *before* the *Nazis* finally invade *both* of them...." He looked at his cigar, his mouth curling downward. "I promised Alma that I'd cut back on cigars due to my heart condition ... but I'm so *overwrought* by all this that I can't seem to stop smoking."

"What about the 'Russkies?' Aren't they going to move to protect their fellow Slavs?"

Alfred Polgar inquired, trying nervously to bite his fingernails, already thoroughly bitten to the quick.

"*Naa*—I just can't see it happening," chimed in Leon Feuchtwanger. "They're hastily rearming, as quickly as they can, but at the same time they won't act *unilaterally*—they want the British and French to move first."

A little over a month-and-a-half later, on a cold and blustery day, came *Kristallnacht*, the notorious 'Night of Broken Glass' throughout Germany. The three dismayed friends shared every nuance of the atrocity with the other residents at the villa. They listened avidly, anxiously, to every radio broadcast from a variety of radio stations. Between them, they spoke or at least understood thirteen languages. They spent the first days after the colossal barbarity listening to constant newscasts about the crisis being inflicted upon their co-religionists in greater Germany.

"*It's worse than anything I could have imagined*," glowered Feuchtwanger, his eyes darting from side to side. "*Thousands* of businesses looted, *hundreds* of synagogues ravaged and burned, *thousands* of Jews arrested and transported to concentration camps, many, many deaths reported—"

"From now on, there cannot be any further delusions… that crazy bastard Hitler and his henchmen are going to kill every Jew that they can get their hands on, but not before robbing them of everything they own…." Alfred Polgar said, his eyes reflecting his

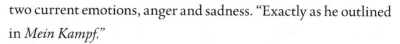

two current emotions, anger and sadness. "Exactly as he outlined in *Mein Kampf.*"

For the next several weeks, things seemed to stumble onward.

Alma mentioned that the situation reminded her of a story she had once heard about the communal methods employed by early Man to provide meat for their tribes.

"They all got together, all the males in the tribe, with spears in their hands, and crept up to a large herd of buffalo. They screamed and hollered and waved their spears, and turned the buffalo toward a nearby cliff. The poor buffalo stampeded, and in their blind panic ran over the precipice…. I think that the Nazis are gathering their modern-day spears right now, getting ready to chase us toward our end."

Superficially, on the surface, things appeared quieter than they actually were. Belatedly, the French and the British began the long slog to re-arm; so too did the Russians. Once 1939 arrived, all crisp and new but tremulous, it didn't take long for the three writers and their fellow residents at the villa to have addition cause for concern.

In January they read and heard about the Spanish Nationalists and their fascist henchmen from Italy gaining control in Barcelona, the final opposition stronghold.

"This is getting too close for comfort," muttered Alfred Polgar. "So now the enemy controls Spain."

In February came the news that British Prime Minister Chamberlain had assured the French that a German attack on France would be considered an invasion of England.

In March the Nazis completed their dismantling of Czechoslovakia with nary a mutter of regret from any of the former guarantors of its independence, England and France.

In April the swirling dark clouds of the impending carnage took on a distinctly sanguinary tinge; Hitler unilaterally repudiated the Anglo-German Naval Agreement as well as the German-Polish Non-Aggression Pact.

Franz Werfel was beside himself with rage.

"Those idiot French and English! Didn't they see this coming? Are they *blind*? You don't need to be a military strategist to see what's going on, and all under the stupid noses of the French and English. The Nazis are now ready to wage war. They've as good as announced it. If I was the president of Poland, I'd be shitting in my pants!"

Polgar looked gaunt and shaken.

"The claxon is sounding for all to hear. It's loud, and it reverberates right under our feet, causing our bones to vibrate and our teeth to rattle."

"But there are still people in important positions among the democracies that are unable to hear it."

"England and France are now standing firm—and so are the Russians. We still have hope of averting war." Alma Werfel sat ladylike on a chaise lounge on the patio, shivering and wishing it were a few degrees warmer.

Lion Feuchtwanger poured some tea for his wife Martha; he looked thoughtful, yet somehow optimistic.

"You know, a few months ago I was in a group of opinion-makers who were invited to have a look at the Maginot Line by the French Ministry of War. I have a great deal of faith in France—but there is, I believe, a *fatal flaw* in the defensive line that they pin so much hope on.... I mentioned it to the general that accompanied us, but he *poo-poo'd* my opinion. He mentioned that 'we have all kinds of deterrents against the Nazis. Besides, he told me that the Maginot defenses are absolutely *impregnable*—"

"So what's the flaw in the French defenses?"

Lion Feuchtwanger leaned forward. "I don't for a moment think that Hitler would attempt to meet the French *head on*... he remembers all too well the months of carnage in those horrible, deathly trenches in the Great War. But more than that ... he also remembers the von Schlieffen plan as well—the quick and deadly right hook through Holland and Belgium, *around* the French defenses, out-flanking them, rendering the whole of the Maginot Line totally *useless*.

"I was told rather haughtily by the general that large elements of the French Army *plus* the British Expeditionary Force were stationed parallel to the Belgian border, all the way up to the English Channel...."

"So wouldn't that prevent the Nazis from invading?"

Feuchtwanger swung his index finger to and fro.

"No, not necessarily. Hitler's not a military genius, far from it.... But this time I believe that Hitler's going to try to do it with *armor.*"

Alfred Polgar scoffed.

"Leon, you obviously have overlooked the terrain up there. There's absolutely no way that tanks can penetrate -"

Feuchtwanger smiled grimly.

"I know that this sounds crazy, with the Ardennes Forest making things difficult for tanks, but von Schlieffen's original idea was to have a holding force on the Russian front, while the bulk of the Nazi Army strikes France with a massive lightning-fast mortal blow—a *blitzkrieg.* And the only way to do that's with tanks."

"*Crazy like a fox!*" exclaimed Franz Werfel.

"Exactly—*Genau!* Crazy like a fox!"

Alfred Polgar interjected. "*But that's impossible.* First of all, there's the point of Dutch and Belgian neutrality. Then there's the *terrain,* the *forests.* Lastly, I don't think that the French and the English are going to sit and allow Hitler to run over the top of them."

"*Remember — he's crazy —* he'll do it! Neutrality never bothered him, and the French sit smugly behind their defensive line, believing that they have Hitler *boxed in*.... Gentlemen — we have to be ready with travel documents in order."

The summer that year was long and hot. With the news growing increasingly grim, the three writers didn't venture too far afield. Trips to Paris became a rarity.

In August came the jarring, astounding news of the Molotov — Ribbentrop Pact. The western allies are caught flatfooted; both Britain and France were busy negotiating with the USSR while Molotov and Ribbentrop announced their bilateral agreement.

"I can't believe it — I'm *speechless!*" exclaimed Franz Werfel. "Who could have guessed that these two *bastards* - ostensibly *sworn* enemies, with completely *opposite* ideologies, would end up in bed together?"

"What do you think are the implications — why were the Russkies and the damned *Nazis* drawn to one another?"

Franz Werfel squinted in concentration.

"Alma read the article to me — her French is far better than mine.... Basically, the Russians had grown tired of the protracted negotiations with the two western powers, and were suspicious of their motives anyway....

"It's as if the Russkies mistrusted Nazi Germany *less* than they mistrusted the Allies; they had warmed up considerably to the

Nazis, who were interested in the USSR as a supplier of necessary raw materials. The Nazis offered the Russians access to German equipment and goods at extremely favorable interest rates. The long-term non-aggression agreement between them was to both their benefits—and besides, they share a deep distrust of western capitalism."

Alfred Polgar grunted.

"There's *got* to be more to it than that—some *hidden protocols* that are mutually beneficial to both."

"Isn't there always?" Lion Feuchtwanger added. "The contorted musings of both Hitler *and Stalin*—I don't think that Kafka *himself* could improve on that, what with his deep mistrust of the State against the little man, the citizen…. Only with Hitler and Stalin, it's *two* warped ideologies pitted against the world…. "Now *there* was a tortured genius of a soul—Kafka—*totally* paranoid and mistrustful."

Feuchtwanger allowed his statement to float before continuing. "I wonder what Kafka would have written about this crazy turn of events." He looked at Polgar, who was nervously rocking his legs. "You knew Kafka, didn't you?"

Alfred Polgar grunted.

"Slightly—we occasionally shared a table at the Café Central on the rare occasions when he visited Vienna…. Such a pity that he died so young."

Even though there were already ominous signs of the impending outbreak of hostilities, the small community of writers and artists sitting on a rocky promontory on the French Riviera, together with the rest of the world outside of Germany, were stunned at what happened next.

The Nazi invasion of Poland, signaling the start of what was to become the Second World War, began just one week later.

The Poles didn't stand a chance.

The *Luftwaffe* pilots had perfected their dive-bombing techniques in Spain, with devastating results. Warsaw and other Polish cities were laid waste.

The *Wehrmacht* overwhelmed the brave but outgunned Polish forces.

Two weeks later, it became apparent to the three writers and to the world at large what at least one of the hidden protocols was: The USSR invaded an already reeling Poland from the east, while western Poland was already in the hands of the Nazis.

With increasing trepidation, the three writers and the others at the villa scanned the newspapers and listened to the various radio broadcasts.

The news was interpreted through filters of personal reflection and empirical knowledge; several of the villa's residents had close family ties to Poland.

"What do you think will happen next?"

"The Nazis and the Russkies are going to finish the job, and then are going to take stock.

"Sure, the Brits and the French have declared war, but apart from U-boat activity at sea, nothing much else seems to be happening."

"The German Navy seems to be winning the battle on the high seas. Those bastard U-boats have sunk a lot of ships—the supply lines to England are being threatened."

Feuchtwanger pursed his lips, a look of disgust on his features.

"My contacts in Paris tell me that the French Army pulled back after '*invading*' German territory because the generals felt that they weren't ready for a full-scale invasion. *What would have been wrong in bartering the return of German territory to the Nazis, in return of French territory to the French*?

"Meanwhile the Royal Air Force was dropping *leaflets* on German cities—if you can believe that! —*Leaflets,* in response to the *Nazi* invasion of Poland! *Who is in charge here*—do they think that this reaction is going to scare Hitler into retreating, into leaving Poland?!"

"Possibly now Hitler will be satisfied with his gains. After all, he can't invade *everybody,* can he?"

"He's made it plain that he wants Germany to rule over all other nations—read his book."

"I think the French can wear him down, even stop him. The Maginot Line can cut German armies up."

"If Hitler comes that way, which he won't"

"Yes, but the French will have lost an opportunity to strengthen their lines opposite the Belgian border. I feel that that's their weakest point. I don't think for a moment that Hitler is going to throw his troops up against the vast defenses of the Maginot Line."

"So you still think that he's going to invade France?"

"*Of course* — and *England as well*, now that he's got the Russians purring like pussy cats."

"We've got to get out of here — what are we waiting for?"

"Where to? *Who'll take us*? Remember the *quotas* — waiting in line, and *still* more waiting… and then *affidavits*… and financial letters of support… and *exit* visas, and *entry* visas. No sooner do we obtain one, after an interminable delay, than the other has already expired. The bureaucracy is *limitless*.…. Join the line and *wait… wait some more* and *hope*."

Time went by: a new decade was ushered in. Nineteen Forty began with a continuation of the 'Sitzkrieg,' or 'Phoney War.'

The Allies were frantically rearming, finally realizing that the *Nazis* were an existential threat, and appeasing Hitler was disastrous.

Several more anxiety-ridden months went by. Both the Allies and the *Nazis* were playing a gigantic game of deathly chess; move and counter-move, on the high seas and then in Scandinavia.

Suddenly Hitler opened with a crushing gambit, to which the Allies had no real counter-response. In the second week of May, he invaded Holland and Belgium.

Franz Werfel looked anxiously at the map on the front page of the newspaper, below the screaming headlines.

"It's obvious what he's trying to do. He's going to go around the French defenses, just as you predicted, Leon. Let's hope that the French and British forces can stand up to him."

The French never recovered from the hammer-blow. Within ten days of the start of the campaign, the Nazis had reached the English Channel; three weeks later Paris fell.

The villa perched on the craggy hill above the azure Mediterranean emptied out while the Nazis swiftly penetrated France. The town too suffered the loss of residents streaming away.

The three writers had no illusions; the two wives urged them on. They realized that the Nazis would come after them and ship them back to Germany to concentration camps as soon as their rule was consolidated in the newly-captured country.

Alfred Polgar was ready first. He'd quickly packed a couple of leather suitcases that showed their age. He waited for Martha and Lion Feuchtwanger to join him in leaving for the port city of Marseille, a short car ride away.

Franz and Alma Werfel demurred, saying that they were immediately leaving for the Spanish border.

"We're going to present them with all the documentation we have, and Alma's going to use all her charm and guile, and pray that that's enough" Werfel said.

Alfred Polgar tried to convince them to join him and the Feuchtwangers.

"Come now—*join us*. There's an American consulate in town—they can help us."

Werfel shot the suggestion down with a hasty wave of his hand.

"Alfred, the roads to Marseille are absolutely *teeming* with refugees seeking shelter from the Nazi *blitzkrieg* up north. Where do you think that many of them are headed once they reach town?"

The Werfels hurriedly rented a car with chauffeur and drove up to the Spanish border in their desperation to get out before the Nazis arrived. Their various documents and their passports didn't pass scrutiny.

After being denied cross-border transit, they eventually found temporary refuge in the nearby pilgrimage town of Lourdes, where Franz Werfel became familiar with the tale of Bernadette, a local teenager who claimed to have seen an apparition of the Virgin Mary in a cleft of rock near the town.

He promised himself that if he and Alma successfully made it to freedom in the U.S., he would write a story based on the apparition. (He later kept his word; his best-selling novel *Song of Bernadette* became the basis for the movie of the same name, starring Jennifer Jones, which won four Academy awards.)

While the Werfels found temporary solace in Lourdes, France signed an armistice agreement with the Nazis. The victors cut France in two; the northern half plus all of the Atlantic coastline was occupied territory. The southern rump down to the Mediterranean became a vassal state, Vichy France, in league with the racist and political aims of the Nazis.

The Werfels eventually joined the masses of refugees looking for a lifeline in Marseille. In the port city, tens of thousands of refugees found the door to freedom locked; the Vichy French were obligated to turn over to the Nazis anyone that appeared to be originally from Germany or from the former Austria.

The Vichy French authorities had enthusiastically endorsed the round-ups, showing a fanatic zeal quite removed from their normal Gallic *bienveillance.*

There was an existential danger of being picked up in the teeming streets of Marseille and being unceremoniously dumped in a Vichy concentration camp to await the inevitable and brutal Nazi vetting process. This process led directly to the cattle cars and shipment to the death camps.

Eventually by word of mouth, many desperate refugees found their way to the Hotel Splendide, to the door of a remarkable American, Varian Fry. A former editor, author and journalist, Fry had seen firsthand how the Nazis treated Jews while on a visit to Berlin in the mid-thirties. He was an eye-witness to anti-Jewish violence during which a man was stabbed to death by laughing, singing storm-troopers.

A Harvard graduate, Fry had also looked up a fellow alumnus, a German-American by the name of Hanfstaengl who had an executive position in the Nazi Propaganda Ministry. The Nazi revealed with casual off-handed comments that Hitler and Goebbels were intent on *exterminating* the Jews, rather than forcing them to emigrate.

Fry was astonished that there were actually leaders of a European country in the twentieth century who would seriously espouse such barbaric actions.

After the fall of France, a motley and diverse group of well-intentioned Americans concerned about the fate of the European cultural and intellectual elite decided that they urgently needed a man on the ground in Marseille to supervise and oversee the relief effort.

Varian Fry volunteered. Initially, the group's objectives were simply to provide relief and some financial assistance wherever necessary to the frantic and despairing refugees.

(Eleanor Roosevelt herself was providing quiet support to the endeavor.)

Fry was supplied with a list of persons whom he should look out for; the original list was greatly expanded once he arrived in Marseille and discovered the horrible truth about the sheer numbers of desperately endangered cultural and political 'enemies' singled out for extermination.

They had all crowded into the port city, hoping against hope for a way out.

Once Varian Fry realized the futility of chasing elusive, expiring visas, contending with invalid passports, battling Vichy French indifference—and worse: they actively obstructed his urgent efforts to save the lives of his hounded *protégés*—he changed tactics.

He decided to use any means possible to rescue people who clamored for his life-saving assistance.

Varian Fry found that the U.S. Consulate staff in Marseille— with one or two notable exceptions—was adamantly opposed to his rescue efforts.

The U.S. Consul, under instructions from Washington, was intent on maintaining friendly relations with Vichy France—the very people who were fully cooperating with the *Nazis*.

Fry was quick to point out to his overworked staff that to merely provide money for food and lodging was playing into the *Nazis'* hands; they were throwing a wide net and were doggedly, efficiently rounding up the beleaguered people that Fry's under-funded group was attempting to save.

Fry began dealing with 'honorary consuls' of certain countries who were amenable to an exchange of money for passports.

He employed a master forger to turn out badly needed documents that stood up to meticulous scrutiny. He dealt in the monetary black market to obtain more favorable rates of exchange.

He defied the dictates of the U.S. State Department; eventually, within a little over a year since his arrival, they and the Vichy French conspired to deport him back to the U.S.

Among the many hundreds of Fry's *'protégés,'* Painter Marc Chagall and his wife, and sculptor Jacques Lipchitz and his spouse were saved, a tribute to Fry's dogged persistence; philosopher Hannah Arendt and husband too were spirited out just ahead of the blood-thirsty Nazis.

The tension and the overcrowding in Marseille grew steadily worse. The Nazis and their French cohorts were harvesting people off the streets whose only crime was to be on a lengthy Nazi 'enemies list.'

One of Fry's able assistants, a wealthy young socialite from New York, Mary Jayne Gold, newly dedicated to rescuing refugees, had rented a villa on the outskirts of the jammed port city to provide their frenetic, paranoid and desperate '*protégés*' with some relief from their extreme anxiety, to give them hope about their very clouded and uncertain futures.

When France capitulated to the *Nazis*, Mary Jayne had been living a high life in Paris; like most of the population, she had badly misjudged the speed at which the Nazis had been able to slice through their country. She fled Paris for Marseille, and eventually, fortuitously, had volunteered to assist in rescuing the hunted refugees from the clutches of the Nazis.

Sitting in the garden of the Mary Jayne Gold's rustic rented villa on a rickety chair, Franz Werfel was in his element. The thing he loved most was holding court — regaling his listeners with stories and reminiscences from his and his wife Alma's travels and adventures.

As the sun was slowly, reluctantly, setting behind the bucolic hills as if battling to stay alive, Franz Werfel pulled out a freshly starched handkerchief and ceremoniously unfolded it on the table in front of him.

His audience in the rented villa's garden watched his every movement, absorbed by his unhurried, methodical action. He palmed the crisp cloth and slowly wiped his expansive, glistening pate. It was a little cooler after the heat of the day; a slight breeze was blowing, but Werfel was a heavy-set man.

The talk around the small garden table laden with food, silverware and bottled drinks was of escape, of leaving, of starting anew in safety and in renewed hope. Many of the people in attendance were already celebrities; others were still to weave their singular thread into the variegated and rich tapestry of life.

Alfred Polgar was also there, as were Heinrich Mann, the essayist and novelist and older brother of Thomas Mann sitting nearby; also Golo Mann, historian and son of Thomas Mann; Andre Breton, father of Surrealist Art; Andre Masson and Max Ernst, both artists; Consuelo de Saint-Exupery, wife of writer Antoine, author of '*The Little Prince*,' plus many family members and loyal staff of Varian Fry's 'American Relief Committee.'

Werfel was whimsical. "At a time like this, I feel it's important to take a deep breath and reflect on the meaning of life, which we all cherish so very deeply.… Life is like a glass of fine champagne. The bubbles tickle your nose as you bring the glass up to your lips.

"Remember to drink it *slowly*, one sip at a time… it's to be *relished*… don't rush it."

He looked around slowly, holding an imaginary glass in his hand. "If you rush it, it'll be *too heady*, too much to handle, isn't that right, Alma?" His wife looked at him evenly, a smile playing on her lips. "Back home, we Viennese have the same feeling about a delicious cup of aromatic *coffee*…one sip at a time, surrounded by good friends."

Franz Werfel smacked his lips at the memory of times spent at his favorite *kaffeehaus*. He looked at his old friend, seated opposite.

"Alfred, what's *your* opinion? After all, you've made a career out of observing and critiquing café-goers."

Alfred Polgar seemed surprised to be called upon. Normally shy and analytical, he preferred to choose when to say something.

He would rather have put his thoughts in writing; he had a biting wit, and his insights were greatly admired for their wisdom and profundity. He once had a reputation for being impeccably dressed, replete with his trademark polka-dot bow tie over a well-starched shirt, tailored jacket and pressed trousers.

In the garden, surrounded by many equally traumatized stateless refugees, Polgar sat forward uneasily on a chaise-longue, his arms uncomfortably pulled around his knees, his shirt wrinkled and open-necked.

He appeared to be what he was—a paranoid, furtive thinker and writer who had been forced out of his element, away from the comforting and cultured ambience he had once known. His lined face and his cautious deep-set eyes reflected the hurt that he felt.

"*Uh*—the Viennese *kaffeekultur* seems so very far away... so *removed* from our existence here.... My old haunt, the *Café Central*, must be on another planet."

He scanned his audience slowly, self-consciously.

"This situation here in Marseille, my friends, reminds me of the African adventure stories I read as a young man. Apparently there's a collecting point on the bank of a wide river over there where wildebeest and gazelles gather to drum up adrenalin and courage—*thousands* of them—before they rush into the crocodile-infested rapids, all in a mad dash to get to the other side and safety....

"The long-snouted reptiles, their huge mouths open in gleeful, greedy expectation of a sumptuous meal wait in the middle to grab them and take them under.... The crocodiles here wear *Nazi* lapel badges on their civilian jackets and coats. They've stowed their black, deathly uniforms and their pistols and machine guns for later use; but *when* and *if* they catch you, *it's over.*"

"Oh, Alfred—*don't be so negative.* "Alma Werfel said, almost pleading. "Mr. Fry is making it possible for us to get out of here—to cross the river you depict—*unharmed.*"

Alfred Polgar smiled wanly.

"Of course, I used a metaphor. We have a border crossing to negotiate, through the *Tunnel of Despair*—that's what I call the thousand-meter-long railway tunnel at Cebère that separates us from Spain, and relative freedom.

"A dark hole carved through the mountain through which the fortunate few can find hope, like so many frantic birds suddenly released from their trapping cage."

Varian Fry chipped in, exuding American confidence and even a bit of naïveté, which his desperate *protégés* found so endearing.

"Folks, it's *do-able*, but it's slightly more complicated than just finding a way through that tunnel.

"First, we have to obtain Vichy French *exit* visas for each individual. Then, concurrently, we have to get the Spanish and the Portuguese to give us *transit* visas…. And remember that each document has an *expiration date*. So if one expires, we have to start the process all over again."

He looked carefully at his rapt listeners, and lowered his voice.

"*If all else fails*, if your available documents aren't completely in order, then we'll have to move you over the Pyrenees Mountains to the other side. It's *illegal*, I realize—but pleading with the Spanish appears to be lots better than remaining stuck here in Nazi-controlled France."

Varian Fry looked like a harried university professor, not at all like someone who in desperation does illegal things to achieve a just objective.

He looked at Alfred Polgar. "So, Alfred—does that give you more hope about your chances?"

The old critic, his weary sad eyes masked by his worried brow, apologized by way of an explanation.

"I've lost my hopefulness about my future. I'm sixty-seven years old—quite a bit older than most of you. I write in the German idiom—the *enemy* language, in the country where we will hopefully be going, The United States of America, our haven on a hill.

"I'm *too old* and incapable of learning English sufficiently well to write with the skill I have in German. So I will have become *useless*."

"Nonsense!" Franz Werfel erupted, more forcefully than he intended. "*Hollywood beckons*... so does *academia*... a nice college in a warm climate... good salary... what more do you want?"

Alfred Polgar's sad eyes filled with tears. "I would like... my old Germany... my former Austria... back... to... what they once... were."

Alma Werfel had been intently following the discussion, together with the rest of the listeners; she interjected. "Unfortunately, this can only happen once the Nazis are... *toppled from power*...."

"And meanwhile the angry black fox is chasing the fat and defenseless hens all over the yard, from coast to coast," said Polgar sadly.

Werfel sensed the dismay that Polgar's metaphor had evoked. He wanted to remind his companions what they were leaving behind, the world where they had grown up and was now viciously attacking them.

"It's true—the *Nazis* have changed Europe, made it into a ferocious beast," he said. "The Europe we have all known and loved is no more.... Progress and enlightenment have been *stifled*, snuffed out.

"We've been *mindlessly* dragged back to the Dark Ages, where vulgar and demonic barbarians now push the rest of us toward flaming pits of death. Or over the cliff, as Alma once described.

"It's not only us *Jews* that are in danger of annihilation—it's the *whole of the civilized world....* "I want to give credence to what is happening here, thanks to the Nazis and Fascism....

"I saw my dear friend Lion Feuchtwanger earlier today, thanks to Miss Gold here. She was able to use her guile and charm— together with considerable bravery—in rescuing Lion from a deathly *cesspool* of a Vichy concentration camp.... His wife Martha is with him, and he's regaining his strength by the minute. It's truly *remarkable* what a little freedom can do...."

Werfel picked up a chipped cup and tipped it gallantly in Mary Jayne's direction.

"Anyway, Lion told me an interesting story, when he and we lived in a little town not far from here, before he and Martha came to Marseille. He was unlucky enough to be picked up as a stateless alien and was sent to a Vichy concentration camp... until today.

"It's about a character—a man of *limited intelligence*—who lived in Lion's old neighborhood in Berlin. Everybody called this man *Schmueli,* even the *goyim.*

"*I'd lived there for years,*" Lion told our group of literary and cultural exiles from *Nazism,* as he poured us lemonade in the villa that we had rented, our temporary haven from the black, berserk brutality coming ever closer.

"'I spent all of my youth in that sheltering, comfortable neighborhood,' Lion recalled, *'until the gusty winds of sudden fame and acclaim caught me and speedily swept me away to a beautiful large house in a leafy suburb....*

"Until the Nazis started hounding me and chasing me down, I used to go back there frequently... just to walk the old, familiar streets so filled with friendly, intrusive ghosts who flitted and swirled around me.

"The bitter-sweet memories of my youth dogged my footsteps, reminding me of my thoughts and feelings across the vanished years.

"Every step I took covered stones that I'd stepped on myriad times before. Every pothole, every tree, every root was known to me. A few of the old crowd still lived there, most of my childhood friends had moved on.

"And, inevitably, there was Schmueli, usually dressed in old, dirty hand-me-downs, the layers of which depended on the season of the year.

"Apart from his graying facial hair, his appearance remained basically the same as when I was just a tike falling over my own shoelaces.

"Schmueli was never overlooked at holiday time. Every homemaker in the neighborhood made sure that he had generous samples of what they cooked or baked.

"Families would always find something extra for him — an old pair of shoes, some discarded article of clothing... sometimes a spare blanket for the bitter cold of winter.

"During the Jewish holidays, Schmueli would inevitably be heard chanting something appropriate and topical as he ambled down the streets.

"The reason for this was that he would stand behind the old shul, and try in his own way to imitate the chants he heard through the open windows of the temple. The voices were fervent and loud, beseeching the Almighty to intercede, but only in His chosen time.

"Where Schmueli slept was open to considerable speculation, with rumors abounding that a wealthy family let him sleep in their warm outhouse.

"Others stated with absolute conviction that he slept downstairs in the storeroom of a large local restaurant, among the dirty tablecloths and serviettes thrown down the chute by the waiters.

"My parents at one time were so concerned during a particularly long freezing spell that they sent us kids out to try to locate him, to offer him a warm place to sleep. But Schmueli was nowhere to be found.

"He never let on where exactly he spent his nights; he was always evasive, always non-committal. It was as if his mind was somewhere far, far away. He played cat-and-mouse with us, never really allowing anyone into his nebulous reality.

'When we were young,' Lion related, 'the neighborhood urchins and I would persist in asking him where he lived, where he slept.

'We just couldn't fathom that he didn't have a home of his own. And in that typical obfuscating way of his, he would lower his eyes, a slight smile playing on his lips. He would say 'I'm saving up to build a big tree-house in the tallest oak tree in the whole neighborhood.'

'Of course, because he was Schmueli, he always changed his answer just to confuse and confound us. Sometimes he would say that he was going to build a tall steel tower to move into. Other times he would point to the top of the tallest building he could see.

"Since we were innocent, gullible kids, we would ask him why he didn't want to live closer to the ground. With a hint of his Kafkaesque thought process, he would say that the earth was where we would all end up, and that he didn't want to hasten the process. He visited the ground, in his own mind, only under protest….'"

Franz Werfel lifted both arms as if to allow some air to reach his armpits; his jacket afforded him little comfort from the heat. He looked deeply into the eyes of his audience, assuring himself that he had everyone's rapt attention.

"Lion continued with his tale. 'When the Nazis came to power, they worked extra hard to impose their diabolic changes, especially in Berlin. Things got steadily worse for the Jews, and, of course, Schmueli suffered as well, along with the rest of us.

"More than likely, he didn't comprehend who exactly these brown-shirted monsters were who ran around yelling and threatening the area residents.

"But he'd suffered discrimination and abuse all his life, due to his limited mental capacity. He must have thought in his own way that things had just gotten worse with the passage of time."

✦

"Several years ago, while on a nostalgic visit to his old neighborhood, Lion heard Schmueli tell the newest generation of neighborhood children what his plans were.

"Schmueli generally had enough acumen to stay out of trouble, but food was getting hard to come by. Severe restrictions had been imposed on the Jewish community.

"By then Schmueli had changed his future housing aspirations to reflect the danger and confused trepidation he felt.

"Lion heard him say that he planned to move into a tree-house and never come down — *not for any reason....*

"The newest generation of children told Schmueli that his plan wouldn't be possible. After all, they reasoned, he had to buy food, and he had to defecate and pass water.

"Wide-eyed children of any age can be oh-so-practical and objective, even as they listened in astonished wonder to the fertile but totally irrational mind of a simpleton like Schmueli.

"I won't come down — I won't. If they try to come up and take me, I'll drop all my shit on them.... I just want to be left alone!"

"The last time Lion was there, in his old neighborhood, filled with so many haunting and cherished memories, he saw some Nazi brutes running after poor Schmueli.

"Lion ran after them, trying to let them know that Schmueli

was just a gentle and blameless old man, who had lived his whole life never harming a fly.

"Lion saw them catch up with him, beat him, kick him, then beat him some more, even after it was obvious that they had badly injured him.

"Lion approached them filled with the horror of the Nazis' brutality. Then they saw Lion, with *his* Semitic features. *And he ran…* Lion ran like he hadn't done in years. Fear had given him wings….

"Lion told me that he still grieves for poor Schmueli, even now, after so much more has happened…. He grieves for the Schmueli of his youth."

Werfel was a pragmatic, driven author — a man with stories to relate. No one in the enveloping gloom saw that, as he removed his glasses with an unnecessary flourish, he stroked away a tear.

Postscript: Well after the war, toward the end of his short life, Varian Fry was nominated a *Chevalier de la Legion d'Honneur* by France, belatedly acknowledging his exceptional bravery and accomplishments in saving over a thousand desperate people from annihilation.

Posthumously, Fry was honored by the Israelis and the U.S. for his selfless, singular humanitarianism. In 1991, then-Secretary of State Warren Christopher gave high praise to Fry's valiant lonely battle, and profusely apologized for his department's and his government's lack of assistance and cooperation at the time of greatest need.

About the Author

Henry Michael Parnes has lived a long life, living and/or working on five continents.

He's an avid reader and long-time writer of novels, short stories, plays and articles, and is the author of *A European Saga* (available on Amazon Kindle). He wrote three-act plays *The Family Farm* and *Their Last Go-around*, and many other shorter plays.

Henry is a proud and active member of the South Florida Writers Association, where he has won many prizes and awards for his work.

He's an active member of the South Florida Theater League, and a long-time resident of South Florida, where he lives happily with his wife Sonia.

Hopefully you'll enjoy the short stories in this book as much as he enjoyed creating them.

The author can be reached at henryparnes@hotmail.com